Spirit, Rhythm, and Story

Community Building and Healing through Song

Terence Elliott

ISBN 978-1-64471-368-6 (Paperback)
ISBN 978-1-64471-369-3 (Hardcover)
ISBN 978-1-64471-370-9 (Digital)

Covenant Books, Inc.
11661 Hwy 707
Murrells Inlet, SC 29576
www.covenantbooks.com

Contents

Preface

Serving Community through Music

Each one, teach one!

—*African Proverb*

*S*erving the community through song is a journey I have been on for most of my life, though I did not always understand that it was community service that I was doing. Growing up in the 1960s in Richmond, California, was an exciting and rewarding experience. I lived in Parchester Village, a historic Black community on the edge of town. There were not many choices for most young Black males in my neighborhood. It seemed that you either participated in sports or music, or in many cases, you did both—as I did. My older brother was indeed the gifted one in our family for games and he chose the athletic road. I tried to pursue that path but, unfortunately, injuries held me back. Music became my *soul alternative*.

The music bug had bitten me at an early age and I wanted to play the piano. I asked my father if he would buy us a piano. Since my first cousins owned one, it seemed only right for us to have one as well. He said no and that if I wanted to play the piano, I could go across the street and practice on the church piano. That did not seem like a fair solution, but my father's other option was for me to get a job. Eventually, I did just that—got a job and bought my first electric piano. I learned a valuable lesson and probably the reason why I still play the piano today.

In high school, I played in school bands and participated in sports—basketball and track. Trombone was the instrument I played in the school marching and concert bands, and by the time I was a senior, I played lead piano in the jazz band. What an accomplishment! During my high school days, I played the electric piano in one of the best *Top 40* groups in the Bay Area—the Establishments. We mainly gigged locally, playing at clubs on various military bases in the area. Although at the time I was not twenty-one years old or the legal age to be in clubs, I already had a full beard, so no one questioned me. The Establishments's big once-a-year gig was playing at the Fresno Relays for the significant dances that happened in the evenings after the track meet. I spent most of my free time practicing the piano or working with bands throughout high school. The values I learned from my musical experiences in high school and local bands were discipline, preparation, and teamwork.

After high school, I attended community college thinking I would major in electronics since I had taken several classes at my high school and that was the career of choice back then. I intended to design and build my own keyboard. I had read that Stevie Wonder had designed the Fender Rhodes electric piano (my first piano), so this is what I wanted to do as well.

Arriving in community college was not quite what I thought it would be. It never felt like I was attending a college, just an extension of my high school. I planned to transfer after a year or two, so I enrolled in the classes one would need to transfer—Algebra, English Composition, Social Science, etc. I also completed my schedule with some music classes—Jazz and Blues Appreciation, Music Theory, and Jazz Piano. I knew after that first semester what I wanted to do with the rest of my life. I was destined to be a musician!

I transferred the next year to San Francisco State University (SFSU). It was 1976, and all the dust and turmoil of the student protests on campus between 1968–1972 was just now clearing. College faculty and staff who had recovered from the trauma were either out for vengeance or appreciating what they helped to change. Transferring to SFSU in just one year was made possible through EOP (Equal Opportunity Program). Getting in was not the hard part; figuring out what to major in was more difficult. I thought I was clear from the start that I wanted to major in music. But after meeting with my advisor and being told I was not the typical music major mainly because I did not have a classical background and never had been officially trained on the piano, I was discouraged and thought about changing my major. The advisor told me that it would take me a long time to complete a music degree, maybe up to ten years, since he thought I was at least ten years behind most of the music majors there. But I felt some of his cultural prejudices and did not know what other college majors I might pursue, so I stayed with music.

In the summer of 1975, the year I graduated from high school, one of the hit songs played on KDIA Lucky 13 radio station was from a jazz musician, John Handy, who was teaching at SFSU at the time. The song was "Hard Work." I was geared to go to SFSU and major in jazz music. Little did I know you were supposed to know how to play at an exceptional level. Auditioning for the jazz band at State with my friends was very disappointing. When it came time for the piano players to try out, there were four of us competing. John Handy, who was one of the reasons why I attended SFSU, only accepted three. I was not one of the lucky ones. I was again at a crossroad. Another lesson learned—it was going to take hard work to be at a professional level and this was not high school; the competition was fierce.

I focused on my studies and worked on improving my piano skills through my undergraduate training. I was fortunate to complete my Bachelor of Arts in Music after only three and a half years at SFSU (although, my music advisor thought it would take me longer). During this period, I was transformed through new encounters and relationships that would forever be part of my life. The communities built from these friendships were my real education and they helped me to become the person I am today.

The following year, in 1980, I decided to remain in school and begin my graduate studies in Ethnomusicology. I applied to UCLA because that was not a major at SFSU. Unfortunately, I was not accepted to UCLA, so I changed my direction to Interdisciplinary

Studies at SFSU, focusing on music production. It was during the summer of 1981 that I had the opportunity to travel to Nigeria, West Africa. This trip was indeed a life-changing experience. I was a member of the Wajumbe Cultural Ensemble. *Wajumbe* is a Swahili term meaning "people who bring a message." Wajumbe was one of the most prominent dance companies in the Bay Area. I heard that at that time, the Bay Area had the most substantial number of Black dance companies in the country. Being in Wajumbe was a big deal and it provided me the chance to travel abroad through music. I became the music director, and my girlfriend—now my wife—was one of the singers and dancers in the company.

The six-week experience in Nigeria was truly mind-boggling. The things I saw and learned were a part of my calling: how African people used music for almost every aspect of life, from washing their clothes to pounding the yam for dinner. The music and dance were so hypnotic. Through continuous drumming and chanting, it was almost impossible not to be connected. All of my experiences up to this point seemed to be connected through music and community: what I am calling community building through song.

Forming communities in college was also a survival strategy. It helped me to develop many friendships and bonds with other musicians, dancers, and artists. Growing up in an all-Black village taught me the importance and significance of community. The friendships I built through sports were not as strong for me as those I developed through music. Something about the power of creating music and song draws you close with others around you.

As an adult, my best friends had become my college companions and musicians. These bands and groups have taught me about companionship, trust, love, commitment, dedication, purpose, joy, and pain. The group that stood out the most was Kuumba Jazz Ensemble, with Mtafiti, Kamau, Amanda (my wife), and Nantambu. Those practice sessions were almost as rewarding as the gigs we did. I had become a cultural revolutionary artist. I received two BA degrees, Black Studies and Music, and a Master's in Interdisciplinary Studies. I was teaching high school at the Emiliano Zapata Street Academy with my best friend, Mtafiti, and about to be married to my college sweetheart—Amanda Hebert.

I taught at the Street Academy for ten years, and close to the end of my tenure, I formed a youth group—Waimbaji. Really, *they* formed this vocal group from a class I was teaching in Richmond. These seven singers were all in high school or had just graduated— three males and four females. Waimbaji was founded upon the principles for which its name translates: song, harmony, and togetherness. The group was formed at the East Bay Center for the Performing Arts (EBCPA). I was the group's director, and this group helped to make a mark for me as music director for Black youth.

The objective of this group was to bring a positive message through song. Waimbaji members dedicated themselves to helping other youths see the difference they could make if they believed in themselves and were committed to doing something productive with their lives.

These talented youth and I composed several original songs and performed them throughout the San Francisco Bay Area for churches, community organizations, schools, and local dignitaries. We also were given the unique privilege to sing the Pan-African People's Anthem, "Nkosi Sikelel iAfrika"—a part of the Bay Area Mass Choir that assembled to perform for the Honorable Nelson Mandela on his historic visit to the United States after being released from serving twenty-six years in prison in June 1990. We had the opportunity to travel with Wajumbe Cultural Ensemble to Nigeria in March 1991. After teaching high school, I entered the community college arena and became a full-time professor and chair of the African American Studies Department at Contra Costa College (CCC) in San Pablo.

The Black Song and Poetry (BSAP) ensemble was a class I formed to guide students in the Black Studies Department at CCC toward becoming more active with their college and community. The class met in the campus one week, and then in the community the next to engage their expressions and use what they were learning by taking African American studies courses with the people in the surrounding areas. I was able to take BSAP to Ghana, in West Africa, for a ten-day performance and study tour.

These experiences have made me the person I am today. I hope you relish reading and learning about how songs are notable for engagement, building, upliftment, unity, education, and healing of the community. Learning some new facts about the songs discussed and the powers of music hopefully will motivate you to sing more, and maybe learn how to play yourself. I hope you will, someday, like me, enjoy your life through song and the magic of its powers.

Asé, Asante, and Alafia Oluwa
Terence "The Professor" Elliott

Chapter 1

Community Songs: Spirit, Rhythm, and Story

Mtu ni Watu! (A person is people.)

$\mathcal{U}$rban communities throughout the United States and the world are in a phase of rebuilding: economically, socially, spiritually, and culturally. It is imperative in these times that the community remembers the values that distinguish it and make it different. In the work to build community, it is valuable to learn how songs can help unite people toward change. The research presented in *Community Building and Healing through Song* will provide information on the histories of songs and their role, effect, and impact on community building efforts toward health and cultural healing. Throughout history, music, storytelling, and songs have drawn groups together. Most special occasions and celebrations include songs, and communities can often be identified by the music they share.

A community is a group of interacting people living close to each other in a common location. The word summons two key concepts: commonality and unity. Therefore, a community is a group of interacting people living in close location to each other, with *shared or common values*. Here is a quote by Bishop Desmond Tutu explaining how each person is tied to another to form communities:

A person is a person through other persons.
None of us comes into the world fully formed. We

> would not know how to think, or walk, or speak, or
> behave as human beings unless we learned it from
> other human beings. We need other human beings
> in order to be human. I am because other people
> are. A person is entitled to a stable community life,
> and the first of these communities is the family.

According to Kimberley Hodgson (2013), the ability to simultaneously preserve and invent a community's culture by conserving its history and heritage and at the same time developing new expressions for current times is a sign of a healthy community. Hodgson further writes that despite the importance of preserving a community's history and heritage, it should also serve as a basis for innovation and advancement. Too often, sufficient resources are not dedicated to preserving spaces to document stories from elders and of a community's contemporary cultural practices. Cultural, artistic, and creative strategies help to reveal and enhance a community's character and sense of place. These elements are all significant in consideration of community interests in decision-making processes, the integration of arts and cultural resources in a civic framework, and the recognition and balancing of the conflicting nature of past, present, and future social values (Hodgson, 2013).

The process of relationship-building that encourages learning and action, as well as the expression of ideas and opinions about a given issue or program, is called community engagement. In planning, community engagement strengthens the level of public commitment and makes more perspectives available to decision-makers. Planners and community leaders have used a variety of traditional tools, such as public opinion surveys, visioning workshops, asset-based planning, town hall meetings, and public hearings to promote and engage the community. Creative tools can serve the same purpose, like visual art techniques, storytelling, festivals, exhibits, dance/spoken word/music performances, web-based applications, and community gatherings which help emphasize receptiveness to input, the honest acknowledgment of feedback, relaxed participation, and the development of people's relationships (Hodgson, 2013).

Communities are increasingly recognizing that the presence of arts and culture in specific neighborhoods can increase attention and attract visitors which may provide a competitive edge by elevating a community's quality of life, thereby improving its ability to attract economic activity and helping create a climate for innovation to flourish. Having formal and informal training in the arts can develop valued skills in the global economy, such as keen oral and written communication skills, high-quality work performance, and the ability to work well with diverse cultures.

Community building is a field of practice directed toward the creation or enhancement of community between individuals within a regional area or common interest. A significant aspect of community building is community service. Community service is rooted in a traditional African legacy of connectedness and intergenerational obligation (Jones, 1998). African metaphysics, according to Jones, emphasized three fundamental aspects of humanity: (1) that individuals and communities have the capacity to celebrate life, even in despairing situations; (2) that individuals and communities are visionaries who have the creative power to manifest their visions; and (3) that individual identity is communal, which the individual operates in a network that provides economic, religious, and political functions. African Americans have a tradition of helping themselves and others in the community. This legacy of self-help and volunteerism has survived throughout the African diaspora. This sense of community aided the transition from slavery to freedom and later supported the Black struggle for liberation. The Black perception of community service remains an extension of traditional African notions of family and community responsibility (Jones, 1998).

The community needs to be trained and oriented to enjoy the arts and appreciate their importance. Art has the ability to educate, entertain, liberate, and cultivate our communities to be more productive and can provide a means for more awareness and pride. Understanding the health and healing aspect of art is another critical priority for community building through song.

The arts should work to create a positive environment and a culture of creativity so as to best improve the health of all people.

Nigerian performing artist Aluede (2006) states that music therapy is the art of using musical sounds to bring changes in a person's unhealthy condition to a more comfortable state. There is no clear evidence of when music therapy first originated, but according to Aluede, it is found throughout African history and still practiced today in all African states. McClellan (1988) has observed how music affects the body through the principle of resonance, but the primary strength of the music is that it works on an emotional level, as well as the spiritual. "The basic premise upon which healing music operates is that a primary cause of disease is emotional stress and negative mental attitudes that create energy imbalances and blockages" (McClellan, 1988, p. 109). Found in the Holy Bible in I Samuel 17:10 is an account of how David played his lyre to heal King Saul's mental problems. Africans believe in the curative properties of music, not just in religious practices but also in their social lives. Aluede (2006) further explains that music is a curative agent in the treatment of psychological and emotional disorders, helping soothe the death of family members and even revive coma patients. Music therapy in Africa is used even to revive a dying person or animal; "to resuscitate a dying person, a single tone of a wind instrument is sounded into the person's ear" (Aluede, 2006). When resuscitating little chicks and other birds, a bowl is placed upside down encircling over the animal during a healing song, with intense drumming on the bowl. Africans believe their minds rule their bodies. Through dancing, singing, and drumming for hours, they bring about community healing and wholeness (Doumbia, 2004).

Beyond Africa, there is a growing community all over the world researching and writing about the efficacious use of musical sounds in healing practices. Paul Twichell, founder of the Eckankar (meaning coworker with God) religious movement and considered a living master, states how the Hu sound (pronounced *hui*) governs the whole universe. From Twichell's view, sounds such as a moving engine, transactions in the marketplace, waterfalls, and oceans all have the Hu sound of life. This Hu sound has been reported to heal, rejuvenate, and invigorate whoever sings it (McClellan, 1988).

One way to have more participation from the community is to share universal values through the singing of songs. Each gathering allows different ethnic groups or random individuals to volunteer to lead and teach a song (or tell a story, recite a poem, etc.). This can be entertaining, as well as educational.

Chapter 2

The Purpose and Power of Songs

Our purpose is to use our creativity and enthusiasm
to support and inspire others as we all freely express
our talents in joyfulness, harmony, and love.
—*Tania Tyler*

The primary approach throughout this book is to investigate how songs have had a resounding impact on humanity. The major focus is on black music and how its songs help the Black community to organize, unite, heal, survive, socialize, and document the *stories of the people.* Understanding how songs have been used to transform the people and community to live in faith, pride, and purpose is the underlying message of the text.

Through the power and magic of the word, or Nommo, man has mastery over all things (Jahn, 1958). The power of Nommo, or word seed, is with its life force. The awareness of how the word alters the world with its force, responsibility, and commitment is African cultural characteristics. A man has to have, through the force of his *word,* dominion over things through changing and making them work for him. To command a thing is to practice magic, according to Jahns, and in practicing word, magic is to write poetry. He further states that to the Yoruba people, the mere word itself does not convey a concept or idea, it must be uttered through man who gives it interpretation and meaning. For the African, the expression of poetry is in the service of the content, not about expressing oneself, but about what must be. This is different from the European poet who is individualistic and expresses what he thinks, feels, has experienced, and wants. The African poet speaks to the community and for them (Jahn, 1958). However, to preserve these lyrical and musical expressions, it was essential to develop methods of documentation.

The song is probably as old as humankind, but the musical notation relied on by musicologists to decipher the oldest known songs is represented by European music and dated as early as the seventh century. Most of the earliest preserved Western music was church music because the church clerics were the main propagators of musical notation during that time (Stevens, 1960). Songs came into existence probably as a means of emotional expression, for a song is not only the birthright of man but also an immediate and satisfying method of expression and an intensification of feeling (Hall, 1953).

A song, in music, is usually a composition for voice or voices performed by singing or by musical instruments. If music is organized sound, then a song is organized sounds which includes rhythm, melody, and sometimes harmony. The rhythm gives the song a beat or meter to initiate movement. A melody is a phrase or line that can be sung or played by an instrument. Harmony can imply that the melody is layered with other voices or instruments, presenting one or more tonal sounds along with the line. Musical instruments may accompany a song or it may be unaccompanied. Most musicologists and scholars will agree that "African music has always been able to translate the experiences of life and the spiritual world into sound, enhancing and celebrating life through cradle songs, songs of reflection, historical songs, fertility songs, songs about death and mourning, and other song varieties" (Floyd, 1995).

There are still many common characteristics shared between African Americans and Africans, especially in the music that has traveled across the ocean in the *souls of men*. Some of these similarities are the solo and chorus type of song where singers and instrumentalists formulate the use of repetition and improvisation. The songs reflect the characteristics of African people, such as dignity, vigor, humor, and depth of feeling (McLaughlin, 1963). The songs and folk stories of the African oral tradition are more than just dates and names that happened in history, they are humanity lessons that narrate a people's sojourn of survival, joys, and sorrows.

African music naturally came out of an African aesthetic, meaning it was viewed as a communal group activity which in itself defines the details of a song. Since it was a collective musical experience, it must have a form or structure where someone leads the song and then the chorus responds. The lyrics and music of these songs were centered around the traditions of African society in which they accompany and are an integral part of activities of daily life. As an example, if people are going to sing while working, then the music needs to be coordinated with the work. The lyrics will reflect the kind of work being done and the rhythms will reflect the kind of pace needed from the workers (Maultsby, 2005), as well as the right mind-set to do the job.

In all traditional and modern African communities, music is a central force. For Africans, the creation of music involves traditional African art elements combined with local social situations and conditions. African music is a constant and clear dimension of African American music, too—not the exact body of works but rather the conceptual approach, as in the *way* of doing something, not merely how something is done (Hester, 2000). It is more about the process of doing things, like performing music. It is not just about the final product or performance but the experience.

African traditional musicians did not seek to combine sounds to please the ear. Their aim was more to express life in all aspects through the medium of sound. The musician was not merely trying to imitate nature utilizing a musical instrument but by taking natural sounds and incorporating them directly into his music. African music can help one understand that what matters is not the quality of the music itself but its ability to render emotions and desires as natural as possible (Bebey, 1975). Music was a way to communicate along with nature and in a communal way. It was not crucial that the music be perfect or played the same way each time; it should be more a reflection of life as it is evolving. A person's life lived out in song, what a thought—like a nonstop musical of the daily events and activities, relationships, aspirations, and defeats.

African music derives from a holistic cultural foundation. Music is culturally confined and a language of culture—like music is an element of culture. The historian Lawrence Levine in his canonical text, *Black Culture and Black Consciousness* which still ranks among the best books written about African American culture, states that "Culture is not a fixed condition but a process: the product of the interaction between the past and present" (Levine, 1977). Levine further suggests that culture's resiliency is not determined by its ability to withstand change but through its ability to react creatively and responsively to current situational realities. In African culture, music is not an isolated art form. It is combined with the visual and kinetic artworks to heighten the total ritual experience. The dress is essential, too, and plays a large role among African people, especially musicians and artists.

There is very little known and understood about the traditional music of the Black peoples of Africa. The music of Africa is rhythmic, vital, and often complicated to external ears. The African harp (2500 B.C.) is considered one of the oldest instruments in the world, but the drum, which some call the *heartbeat* of Africa, is the most talked about (Afrika, 2004). The drum is still associated with a means of communication in many areas of Africa today, and it has a special place in ceremonies of state, in rituals, in festivals, and even in litigation.

A critical excerpt below is from one of the oldest manuscripts on the music of enslaved Africans, *Slave Songs in the United States*, which was published in 1867 by Simpson and Company.

> The voices of the colored people have a
> peculiar quality that nothing can imitate; and the
> intonations and delicate variations of even one
> singer cannot be reproduced on paper. There is
> no singing in *parts*, as we understand it, and yet
> no two appear to be singing the same thing, the
> leading singer starts the words of each verse, often

improvising, and the others, who base him, as it is called, strike in with the refrain, or even join in the solo, when the words are familiar. When the base begins, the leader often stops, leaving the rest of his words to be guessed at, or it may be they are taken up by one of the other singers. And the basers themselves seem to follow their own whims, beginning when they please and leaving off when they please, striking an octave above or below (in case they have pitched the tune too low or too high), or hitting some other note that chords, so as to produce the effect of a marvelous complication and variety, and yet with the most perfect time, and rarely with any discord. And what makes it all the harder to unravel a thread of melody out of this strange network is that, like birds, they seem not infrequently to strike sounds that cannot be precisely represented by the gamut, and abound in slides from one note to another, and turns and cadences not in articulated notes. It is difficult to express the entire character of the Negro ballads by mere musical notes and signs. The odd turns made in the throat, and the curious rhythmic effect produced by single voices chiming in at different irregular intervals, seem almost as impossible to place on the score as the singing of birds or the tones of an Æolian Harp. There are also apparent irregularities in the time, which it is no less difficult to express accurately.

Enslaved Africans in America were not allowed to read or write and were mainly here for labor, so the oral traditions brought from Africa to America were sustained. Transmitting history, legends, cultural information, and the current news was done easily through songs, whether it was on the field working, Sunday church services, or in the cabins before they fell asleep. Since most enslaved Africans were denied access to musical instruments, the voice was often the primary method of music making. If there were instruments to play, such as the banjo or the fiddle or maybe even a drum or percussion device, men usually played them. Women, on the other hand, usually were the leaders of the song because many of those songs alluded to African attitudes and practices. These women with high soprano voices were less threatening to the White masters of the plantation and their voices were more capable of penetrating the rhythmic intensity of the drums and low-pitched male voices. The female voice, throughout the evolution of African American music, has been the guiding force in establishing the stylistic features that eventually fostered the development of spirituals, blues, and jazz (Hester, 2000).

This next section focuses on understanding the main components of a song through its power elements—spirit, rhythm, and story—and how these elements helped to define the various styles and movements of the people.

The term *spirit* relates to how Africans connect to Olodumare, God, Allah, Yahweh, Jehovah, Buddha, the Most Divine, the Higher Being, or whatever the name may be. Belief, fear, and obedience in God are natural with African people. According to Mbiti (1969), in all African societies, the people have a minimal and fundamental idea about God, for Africans know God as High God, a Supreme God, and Father, or, depending on the society, as Mother. They believe God is the Creator and Provider, and they are expected to be humble, respectful, and honorable toward him (Floyd, 1995). In religion and spirituality, the respiration of a human is linked with the spirit, the very occurrence of life. In this sense, spirit means the thing that separates a living body from a corpse and usually implies intelligence, consciousness, and sentience. The word *spirit* is from the Latin *spiritus*, which means "breath" and from a Proto-Indo-European *(s)peis*, which implies the *soul*. Spirit relates to art, or more particularly to a song, as the breath and soul that gives the song that ability to move one and others. It is like what the Yoruba people (from Nigeria) mean by the word *áse* (or spelled *áshe*). When a work of art has *áse*, it transcends ordinary questions about its makeup: it is an incarnated force of divinity. Even words can be transposed into spirit-invoking and predictive experiences, for *ase* means "So be it" "May it happen." It gives art/song the power of life which can heal people, teach them, or make them want to shout, clap their hands, and move their feet. It is what Black people use to refer to as having *soul power.* Master drummer and dancer Dr. Doumbia has written that the universal languages of spirit are music and dance which communicates its poetry through celebration, initiation, and healing. Through the repetitious rhythm playing of musical instruments, song chanting, and dancing, they become in tune with the universe's harmonious vibrations. The drummer, dancer, and singer are taken over by the spirit (Doumbia, 2004).

While the spirit of music relates to its divine qualities, the *rhythm* of art and music relates to the physical aspects of life, especially movement. African ceremonies are not just communications with spirits, but also with one another. Drummers interpret the dancers' bodies and movements with their rhythms, and dancers feel the rhythms and interpret them with their movements. There is a dialogue with one another. Master drummers can dance well, and accomplished dancers know and can play the rhythms of the dance. The various professions (ex. farmers, hunters, blacksmiths) have their own music and dance, too. The workers play music with their work to increase the satisfaction and productivity (Doumbia, 2004). The rhythm for African dance music is in three which is also based on the beats of the heart: "(1) the heart valve open is the first beat; (2) when the heart pauses is the second beat; (3) when the heart valve closes is the third" (Afrika, 2004). *Rhythm* generally is defined as "any regular recurring motion, symmetry, a movement marked by the regulated succession of strong and weak elements, or of opposite or different conditions." For performance art, "rhythm is the timing of events on a human scale; musical sounds and silences, of steps of a dance, or the meter of spoken language and poetry" (Jirousek, 1995, p. 2). There are hundreds of different rhythms that West African musicians know how to play and they know how to use the drum to speak the meanings of the rhythms. For each rhythm has its own story, and for particular rhythms, people are more susceptible than others in how the spirit provokes them (Doumbia, 2004).

The story element of music combines all the other components to evoke a deep feeling or emotion. Stories are told through the music, revealing the histories and the purpose of the people (Doumbia, 2004). According to Bruce Jackson, author of *The Story is True*, the details of real life are clutter, noise, and chaos without informing ideas. Stories are these ideas that give form and breath (Jackson, 2007). Stories are an essential aspect of culture. Flanagan states that humans from all cultures have cast their own identity in some form of a narrative story (Flanagan, 1998). Stories are a needed component of human communication and are usually found in all aspects of art, especially in songs. In most cases, the more information, background, or story is known about a song, the deeper the meaning.

Usually, the non-African listener will generally find African music strange and difficult to follow. After listening to some examples of traditional African instrumental, vocal, and drum music, try answering the following questions:

- What is the power in this music?
- What is an artist's responsibility to the community?
- How is music a way of life?
- How does this music help to give a better understanding of an African's view of art and culture?

Chapter 3

Voices of the People: Spirituals and Freedom Songs

Music speaks louder than words.

—African Proverb

The first songs that the enslaved Africans brought forcibly to America sang were songs from Africa. However, because of fear of rebellions, enslavers prohibited Africans from speaking in their language and playing on African instruments. So the most significant songs in the pre-Civil War period were of a religious nature, or spirituals. Karenga views spirituals as "essential expressions of social strivings and struggle whose themes are: 1) the desire for freedom, justice, and penalty for the oppressor; 2) criticism of the existing order; and 3) coded messages of escape, meetings, and struggle. Some of these song examples are: 'Go Down, Moses,' 'Swing Low Sweet Chariot,' 'Oh Freedom,' 'My Lord Delivered Daniel,' and 'No More Auction Block For Me'" (Karenga, 2002, p. 474). One spiritual especially recognized for having messages of escape was "Steal Away." Notice some of its messages about the time to escape—*in the midnight hour*; the *thunder* could represent the rainstorm (a good time to escape) and the trumpet sound could be the train horn:

Steal away. Steal away.
Steal away to Jesus.

24

Steal away (Steal home); Steal away home.
I haven't got long to stay here.

My Lord, my Lord, He calls me (Calls me); He
    calls me by the thunder.
The trumpet sounds way down in my sanctified
    soul.
I haven't got long to stay here.

Steal away (in the midnight hour); Steal away.
    (When you need some power)
Steal away (when you heart is heavy); Steal away
    to Jesus. (Steal away to Jesus)
Steal away (steal away home); Steal away home.
    (Haven't got long)
I haven't got long to stay here.

My Lord, He calls me (calls me); I can hear Him
    calling me by the lightning (lightnin')
The trumpet sounds within my soul.
I haven't got long to stay here
(Written by Wallace Willis, Choctaw freedman,
before 1862)

These religious slave songs that some call spirituals have a direct
link to hymns: songs of adoration and praise to God. During the
early Christian era, the term *hymns* applied to all songs in praise of
the Lord (Apel, 1977) and sung by the congregation (Hindley, 1976).
Before 1730, Gregorian chants, including psalms and canticles singing, was what the congregation used mostly in the colonial churches
of the United States (Cleveland, 1981). Africans and Blacks, enslaved
or free, generally worshipped in churches with Whites and sang the
same music. During this era, religious instruction for both Whites
and Blacks was an essential prerequisite for membership in the
church and a fundamental part of daily life. The level of instruction
for Blacks in the South was not at all equivalent to the North, and

at no time did it reach a sizeable Black population, either. Despite these Southern laws prohibiting the assembling of Blacks, enslaved Africans would still manage to hold these religious meetings in secret, or at *invisible churches* as they were called, since they were hidden from plain sight (Southern, 1971).

The Great Awakening movement of the 1730s brought a demand for livelier songs in the worship service than the psalms and canticles. This new livelier style of music was called *hymns*. The texts for these hymns were more appealing to Blacks due to the vitality of the words, more extensive use of intervals, and their rhythmic freedom (Southern, 1971).

By the end of the eighteenth century, many Blacks began to disconnect from the White congregations and build their own places of worship. The worship services for these new Black churches had semblances of the White church format. However, the music was performed out of their own indigenous experiences. The new musical forms that arose became known as the Black hymn and spiritual (Cleveland, 1981).

An integral aspect of the Black church has always been music, especially singing. As Blacks established their churches, they did not discard their experiences in White Christian worship, such as singing hymns, but adopted and converted these hymns into original Black songs. These hymns developed from diverse influences, including: "(1) African religious music, (2) the African call and response song, (3) European or American religious and secular songs, and (4) various African and African American dialects" (Cleveland, 1981).

One of the classic hymns that has brought much comfort to Black people is "Amazing Grace." This song was composed by a former slave trader, John Newton, who dropped out of school at age eleven and became a seaman and, eventually, a captain of a slave ship. Newton was known to have engaged trade and ferrying of African people under vile conditions. He converted to Christianity after being terrified by a storm and having emotional guilt. Then Newton studied for the ministry and became a powerful preacher. To augment his salary as a minister, he composed hymns, one of which was "Amazing Grace."

Another one of America's most prolific ministers and hymn writers was the renowned Dr. Charles Albert Tindley (1856–1933) who, for more than thirty years, was the pastor of the famous East Calvary Methodist Episcopal Church in Philadelphia, Pennsylvania. As a composer, Dr. Tindley's most productive period was from 1901–1906, although his music was not popular in Black (Negro) churches until after World War I. Dr. Thomas Dorsey, one of the greatest Black gospel/spiritual composers, expressed how it was the music of Dr. Tindley that inspired him to leave the vaudeville and blues circuits and exclusively write religious music. It was a refrain to a Tindley hymn that transformed into the greatest of all freedom songs:

Original version:

> I'll overcome someday; I'll overcome someday;
> If in my heart I do not yield, I'll overcome someday.
> (From the Black hymn, "I'll Overcome Some Day")

Transformed version:

> We shall overcome, we shall overcome
> We shall overcome some day
> Oh, if in our hearts, we do not yield,
> We shall overcome someday.
> (From the freedom song, "We Shall Overcome")

Dr. Tindley was an outstanding and world-renowned minister who not only ministered through the spoken word but through song. His numerous hymns remain a legacy that will live on and on. Even though Tindley's gospel hymns grew out of the Black experience, they still possess strong universal appeal and remain useful to all races (Cleveland, 1981).

When the term *spiritual* was first applied to the religious folk songs of Blacks is not known but it must have been in common usage by the 1860s. The editors of *Slave Songs of the United States* used the term *spiritual* (or *sperichil*) in the introduction without defining it.

Through the years, Blacks have developed a repertory of religious songs away from the surveillance of Whites in their independent Black churches, segregated camp and bush meetings, and neighboring plantations in hiding or secret places for worship. Ideationally, spirituals were classified the same way as secular songs. They had spirituals for singing in the church worship service, for singing while just sitting around, and for singing to accompany the shout—as in *ring spirituals*, *shout spirituals*, and spirituals for funeral singing (Allen, Ware, and Garrison, 1867).

The earliest link between the newly imposed Christianity of enslaved Africans and their past is the shout. The name even bears semblance with an African term *saut*. The *s* sounded as *sh* that describes the same ring-shout pattern. The shout is still practiced today and its elements still arise in gospel and rhythm and blues songs. The ever-continuous repetition of a bass line or a chant with an upbeat groove to it can get people in a very hypnotic state. Here is another excerpt from the text *Slave Songs* which does a great job describing a shout.

> The true 'shout' takes place on Sundays or on 'praise'-nights through the week, and either in the praise-house or in some cabin in which a regular religious meeting has been held. Very likely more than half the population of the plantation is gathered together. For some time one can hear, though at a good distance, the vociferous exhortation or prayer of the presiding elder or of the brother who has a gift that way, and who is not 'on the back seat,'—a phrase, the interpretation of which is, 'under the censure of the church authorities for bad behavior;'—and at regular intervals one bears the elder 'deaconing' a hymn-book hymn, which is sung two lines at a time, and whose wailing cadences, borne on the night air, are indescribably melancholy. But the benches are pushed back to the wall when

the formal meeting is over, and old and young, men and women, sprucely-dressed young men, grotesquely half-clad field-hands---the women generally with gay handkerchiefs twisted about their heads and with short skirts---boys with tattered shirts and men's trousers, young girls barefooted, all stand up in the middle of the floor, and when the 'sperichil' is struck up, begin first walking and by-and-by shuffling round, one after the other, in a ring. The foot is hardly taken from the floor, and the progression is mainly due to a jerking, hitching motion, which agitates the entire shouter, and soon brings out streams of perspiration. (Simpson, 1867)

The most critical link to African burial ceremonies is the ring or circle which can be traced back to West Africa. The people of West Africa have transformative and multidimensional practices that happen in a circle. The dancers move counterclockwise with their feet close to the ground, with *jerking* or *hitching* motions, particularly in the shoulders. This counter-movement is similar to stopping or opening the ceremony. During this time spirits are allowed to come in and out of dimension. In *Slave Culture*, Stuckey (1987) presents that "the ring shout was the main context in which transplanted Africans recognized values common to them" (p. 16). These values consisted of communication and teaching through storytelling and ancestor worship. In the Americas, Africans would play drums, sing, and dance all day in the cemetery—a common practice in New Orleans and the Georgia Sea Islands. These movements were usually accompanied by a spiritual sung by lead singers, with others in the group joining in and probably adding handclapping and knee slapping. The ring shout was considered by some as an early Negro *holy dance* in which circling about is the essential prime element (Gordon, 1981, p447).

These ring shouts or holy dances can also be quiet as they shuffle; while they sing the chorus of the spiritual, the dancers may also join in and sing. Generally, a band composed of some of the best singers and seasoned shouters stands at one side of the room as a base for others, singing the body of the song and clapping their hands together or on the knees. These songs and dances are usually extremely energetic and will last a very long time, often into the middle of the night (Simpson, 1867).

The ring shout was not to be construed under any circumstance as a dance, and the rules to distinguish between shouting and dancing were strictly observed. For instance, only songs of religious nature were sung, the feet must never cross, and, with devotees, the feet must never lift from the ground. However, there is argument, according to Stuckey (1987), that *shout* is used as a part of the two-word phrase *ring shout* because Whites regarded dancing as vulgar and sinful. For the Negro, the spiritual is central to the ring shout and subsequent to all African American music-making (Floyd, 1991).

A *ring spiritual* was a song that was sung and repeated over and over while the shouters moved around in a circle or ring. This ritual performance would last as long as four or five continuous hours and the song would become more like a chant in character—a fierce, monotonous chant with a repetition of an incoherent cries. The spiritual songs most associated with the shout were: "Oh, We'll Walk Around the Fountain," "The Bells Done Ring," "Pray All the Members," and "I Can't Stay Behind" (Southern, 1971).

Another style of African American religious singing that had strong connection to African tradition was referred to as moaning, which does not imply pain. It is more like a blissful rendition of a song, often combined with humming and spontaneous melodic variation. In various regions of Africa, moaning was used to produce emotion, particularly at funerals in early Egypt (Kemet) and still today in Nigeria. Also, there are singers whose duty is to make folks cry, as those tears enable a deceased person to travel in the afterworld. Moaning, or what Andrew Legg (2010) refers to as the *gospel moan,* is full of emotion and meaning, including a resonance which is more than a physical sound. The moan has a multifaceted and expressive quality that depends on the performer and context, which may range from a closed-mouth, resonating sound through the nasal passage to an open-throated, open-mouthed sound which is louder and more resonant, more akin to a cry of physical pain. Great gospel/soul singers Mahalia Jackson and Aretha Franklin employed the closed-mouth technique when singing over an extended phrase length (Legg, 2010). For Africans in America, moaning is often used in the background to accompany the minister's prayer—a powerful device used to touch the spirit. It is the sound that many Black mothers make when they are feeling down or sad. This moaning sound is infectious. It is a style of singing that helps to express deep, inner emotion. The author remembers how his mother employed this moaning technique as she cried out hymns, singing and working around the house. Hearing this sound of her moaning was sadder than hearing her cry.

Black people sang of the new promise and the new day. Spirituals and other Black songs not only have a great sense of divine power, divine intervention, and of freeing the enslaved, but lay out the mission for the future and celebrate becoming as a people and as a nation (Belafonte, 2001). Paul Robeson once said, "The purpose of art is not just to show life as it is, but also to show life as it should be" (Belafonte, 2001, p. 20). Reflected in the Black voice is the beauty and richness that tells the story of the evolution and quest for freedom.

Anthems

Music of the African diaspora has various functions: a method of rebellion, of revolution, and of defense. It is key to understanding that music is a system of complexity that can mediate our relationships to each other and to our histories. So a *Community Song* is not just its rhythms or danceable beat, it connects people to collective action and a new political agenda. The most central example of a community song is an *anthem*. These anthems blur the delineation between art and politics for the listener and participant. The word *anthem* derives from an ancient traditional term *antiphon* which is the call and response at the core of the twentieth-century Black music movement, whether as a response to God or state formation.

Anthems are a part of the interdisciplinary cultural history using texts composed of set popular musical forms and organizing strategies within the Black movement that are bound together by African-derived performance techniques. As a movement strategy, anthems had first to be practiced among its members. Within these movement organizations, collectively singing and listening was a method of participation for freedom and liberation (Redmond, 2014).

In the civil rights movement, most of the singing was congregational and unrehearsed, as was practiced in the tradition of the African American folk church. The repertoire of core songs was performed in the older style of singing and expanded to include most of the popular African American music forms and singing techniques of that era. During this time, spiritual lyrics transformed by the activist song leaders, traditional melodies used, and methods associated with old forms were blended with new forms to create songs with the force and intent of this freedom rights movement.

From Slave Spiritual to Civil Rights Movement
Freedom Song: Illustrative Examples

Original Slave Spiritual	Civil Rights Movement Freedom Song
Woke up this morning with my mind stayed on Jesus…	Woke up this morning with my mind stayed on freedom…
Don't you let nobody turn you 'round…	Ain't gonna let nobody turn me 'round…
Go tell it on the mountain that Jesus Christ was born…	Go tell it on the mountain to let my people go…
I shall not, I shall not be moved…	We shall not, we shall not be moved…
Keep your hand on the plow, hold on…	Keep your eyes on the prize, hold on…

Over my head, I see Jesus in the air…	Over my head, I see freedom in the air…
This little light of mine, I'm gonna let it shine…	This little light of mine, I'm gonna let it shine…

http://ctl.du.edu/spirituals/freedom/civil.cfm

One should not think about freedom songs from the civil rights movement as if the movement created them strategically. These songs were a natural outpouring—evidence of the life force of the fight for freedom. Many people put their everyday lives at risk to fight racism in their local community. These people belonged to a Black culture that had a very high place for music that they created as a part of their daily lives. Most of the participants from these local communities appreciated music from various genres which they enjoyed not only to listen to but also to sing. They did not just practice one kind of music (Reagon, 1990).

An interesting point about most of these freedom songs is that they function in the movement as *congregational* songs. A song leader begins the congregational songs and a song leader is different from a soloist. A soloist is someone who can execute the entire song. A song leader only starts the song, and if that performance is successful, it is successful not only because of the prowess of the leader but also because of the people that join in to raise the song into life (Reagon, 1990). For African Americans, singing evolved into a cultural strength because a *song* was necessary and reinforced in the churches and other venues for Black expression (Sanger, 1995). When listening to the recordings of the mass *freedom riders* meetings, you will often find people singing, like how everybody in the church would sing. This is congregational singing—the kind of singing done in the Black church, in Black schools, and Black neighborhoods. Sometimes the congregational style of singing was used even for secular activities, rallies where there was a song leader and everybody joined in the singing.

Perhaps the most celebrated of all the freedom songs is "We Shall Overcome." This song was adopted as a kind of unofficial anthem for the civil rights movement and reveals much about the improvisational and hybrid nature, not just of African American musical culture but also of the movement itself. These lyrics derived from Charles Tindley's gospel song "I'll Overcome Some Day" written in 1900, and parts of the melody from the nineteenth-century spiritual "No More Auction Block for Me," a song dated back to before the Civil War. "We Shall Overcome" was adapted from these gospel songs by Guy and Candy Carawan and a couple of other people affiliated with the Highlander Research and Education Center in Tennessee (Southern, 1971). "We Shall Overcome" was first used as a protest song in 1945 when striking tobacco workers in Charleston, South Carolina, sang it on their picket line. By the 1950s, young activists of the African American civil rights movement had discovered the song and decided to implement it as the movement's unofficial anthem.

The song "We Will Overcome" was published in September 1948 in an issue of the *People's Songs Bulletin* (a publication of People's Songs, an organization of which Pete Seeger was the director and guiding spirit).

> We shall overcome, we shall overcome,
> We shall overcome someday;
> Oh, deep in my heart, I do believe,
> We shall overcome someday.
>
> The Lord will see us through, The Lord will see
>   us through,
> The Lord will see us through someday;
> Oh, deep in my heart, I do believe,
> We shall overcome someday.
>
> We're on to victory, We're on to victory,
> We're on to victory someday;
> Oh, deep in my heart, I do believe,
> We're on to victory someday.
>
> We'll walk hand in hand, we'll walk hand in hand,
> We'll walk hand in hand someday;
> Oh, deep in my heart, I do believe,
> We'll walk hand in hand someday.

We are not afraid, we are not afraid,
We are not afraid today;
Oh, deep in my heart, I do believe,
We are not afraid today.

The truth shall make us free, the truth shall make
    us free,
The truth shall make us free someday;
Oh, deep in my heart, I do believe,
The truth shall make us free someday.

We shall live in peace, we shall live in peace,
We shall live in peace someday;
Oh, deep in my heart, I do believe,
We shall live in peace someday.
(A publication of People's Songs, 1947)

The hymn and song anthem "Lift Every Voice and Sing," which was first written as a poem, has had an enormous impact on African Americans and continues to have universal appeal. The genesis of "Lift Ev'ry (original spelling) Voice and Sing," like so much Black music, was locally situated in response to the needs of a particular community. The song was created by James Weldon Johnson and performed for the first time by 500 school children in celebration of President Lincoln's birthday on February 12, 1900, in Jacksonville, Florida. Johnson's brother, John Rosamond Johnson, set the poem to music. In composing the lyrics, James Weldon Johnson noted that the spirit of the poem had taken hold of him. As he paced back and forth on his front porch, he experienced the "transports of the poet's ecstasy" (Johnson, J. W., 1933, pp. 154–155) and could not keep back the tears. This song was written during a time in America in which restraints on African Americans ordained by Jim Crow laws, feverish lynching, and mob violence were a way of life. Yet Johnson's lyrics did not fuel the fires of racial hatred but showed an acceptance for the past and confidence in the future.

A closer look at James Weldon Johnson's biography may help us to understand the kind of person he was to be able to write such profound and provocative lyrics. Johnson was born June 17, 1871, to James and Helen Louise Dillet Johnson, in Jacksonville, Florida. His parents instilled in him and his younger brother, J. Rosamond Johnson, that they could do whatever their young minds could conceive. James even proclaimed as a young child that he wanted to be governor of his home state of Florida. Johnson indeed had the self-confidence and belief that all the privileges afforded to any American citizen. He had the potential, as well. But while attending Atlanta University, he realized that the Jim Crow segregation system did not allow status or individual recognition for African Americans. James Weldon Johnson still had the fortitude and determination not to let hatred or racism stand in his way for righteousness and the good of humanity. Music was his historical artifact that best described the pain and glory for the Black oppressed race (Redmond, 2014).

The National Association for the Advancement of Colored People (NAACP) adopted "Lift Every Voice and Sing" in the 1950s and it is still their official song. James Weldon Johnson was the chief executive officer at the time when the organization adopted it. Johnson declared that he wrote the song as a hymn and not as an anthem, and that a country could only have one national anthem. He did understand, though, that African Americans needed to make the song their anthem of hope and prayer (Bond, 2000). Now "Lift Every Voice and Sing" is one of the most cherished songs for African Americans and is indeed referred to as the Black national anthem. Below is a copy of the lyrics:

Lift Every Voice and Sing

> Lift every voice and sing
> Till earth and heaven ring,
> Ring with the harmonies of Liberty;
> Let our rejoicing rise
> High as the listening skies,
> Let it resound loud as the rolling sea.
> Sing a song full of the faith that the dark past has
> taught us,

Sing a song full of the hope that the present has
    brought us,
Facing the rising sun of our new day begun
Let us march on till victory is won.

Stony the road we trod,
Bitter the chastening rod,
Felt in the days when hope unborn had died;
Yet with a steady beat,
Have not our weary feet
Come to the place for which our fathers sighed?
We have come over a way that with tears has been
    watered,
We have come, treading our path through the
    blood of the slaughtered,
Out from the gloomy past,
Till now we stand at last
Where the white gleam of our bright star is cast.

God of our weary years,
God of our silent tears,
Thou who has brought us thus far on the way;
Thou who has by Thy might led us into the light,
Keep us forever in the path, we pray.
Lest our feet stray from the places, our God,
    where we met Thee,
Lest, our hearts drunk with the wine of the world,
    we forget Thee;
Shadowed beneath Thy hand,
May we forever stand?
True to our God,
True to our native land.
(Written as a poem by James Weldon Johnson
in 1900, and set to music by his brother John
Rosamond Johnson in 1905)

The framing of images through song lyrics, harmonies, and melodies is an excellent method for identifying historic events. Johannes Fabian (1996: 226–277) identifies this as a remembrance of the present. These songs connect to the community where they are performed, imbuing it with their message of historical, social, and political understanding. In Africa, the South African national anthem "Nkosi Sikelel iAfrika" (God Bless Africa) has gained this same kind of mutual respect and acceptance, as well as among people of African descent throughout the world. It was also written as a hymn in the form of a blessing, offering a message of unity and strength. In 1897, Enoch M. Sontonga, a Methodist missionary schoolteacher from Johannesburg, South Africa, composed the hymn as part of a group of songs for the students in his school. Sontonga originally wrote the lyrics in Xhosa, his tribal language. Besides being a teacher, Sontonga was an accomplished poet, composer, choirmaster, lay preacher for the church, and amateur photographer. He actually wrote the first verse and chorus at the age of twenty-four, and later that year composed the music. "Nkosi" was sung on January 8, 1912, seven years after the death of Enoch Sontonga, to the South African Native National Congress by the Ohlange Institute Choir, and in 1925, after changing their name to the African National Congress (ANC), the song was adopted as their official anthem and had to be sung at the close of all their meetings. Copeland writes that "Nkosi Sikelel iAfrika" has come to symbolize, more than any other piece of expressive culture, the struggle for African unity and liberation in South Africa" (Copeland, 1985: 46). The song also symbolized the fight against apartheid which made (Black) Africans aliens in their land, forced to live in rural townships where there was no plumbing, running water, or electricity. For over forty years, Blacks fought back the White supremacy apartheid government system, initially as a nonviolent protest, but eventually through violence. Throughout the struggle, there was the music. The song "Nkosi Sikelel" was able to communicate to people all over the world, and even to the Whites in South Africa, how Blacks felt and how apartheid had to end. Songs like this seem to provoke more of an emotional appeal to people than political speeches or nonviolent protest. Somehow, songs from the oppressed can reach in the soul and spirit of the oppressor to help them understand what the people feel and where they are coming from.

Lyrics to: *Nkosi Sikelel IAfrika*

Nkosi sikelel' iAfrika (*Xhosa*)	God [Lord] bless Africa
Maluphakanyisw' uphondo lwayo, (*Xhosa*)	May her glory be lifted high
Yizwa imithandazo yethu, (*Zulu*)	Hear our petitions
Nkosi sikelela, thina lusapho lwayo. (*Zulu*)	God bless us, Your children
Morena boloka setjhaba sa heso,	God we ask You to protect our nation
O fedise dintwa le matshwenyeho,	Intervene and end all conflicts
O se boloke, O se boloke setjhaba sa heso,	Protect us, protect our nation, our
Setjhaba sa, South Afrika (by Enoch M.	nation,
Sontonga, 1897).	South Africa

Songs like "Lift Every Voice," "We Shall Overcome," and "Nkosi Sikelel" are excellent examples of how communities were built—for strength and courage, pride and dignity, for remembering the past and the promise of the future. These songs are considered anthems which describe a secure connection between the people and the communities they built. The traditional meaning of the term *anthem* is a specific form of angelic church music, but the more general understanding is a celebratory song used as a symbol for a particular group of people. From a music theory aspect, anthems are usually simple melodies where the harmonic structure moves together, and not in polyphony where parts move separately: a song in the harmonic structure that has the lead voice, often the soprano or higher pitch, carry the tune, and the other voices accompany in harmony the underlying melody (Huray, 1980). Singing in a harmonic style is a natural form to learn and to sing along with which is probably why most communities favor these types of songs.

The National Association for the Advancement of Colored People (NAACP) was founded during the post-Reconstruction era and the song they used as a call for justice and liberty was "Lift Every Voice and Sing." The civil rights movement gained much of its popularity and support through the freedom Songs. The *Freedom Riders*, who were young adults risking their lives to protest, march, sit in, and to do vote registrations for the betterment of the quality of life for African Americans, were able to find strength, unity, hope, faith, and dignity through the songs they sang. Most of these songs were *makeovers* from traditional spirituals they sang in church, though some were from popular songs of the day, changing words when needed to fit their cause. The song "Nkosi Sikelel iAfrika" gave people a purpose and voice to continue to fight and have hope. These songs of freedom, including "Lift Every Voice" and "We Shall Overcome," have helped struggle against the ills of humanity all over the world. Many Africans and African Americans know and have sung at least one of these songs discussed above, either from growing up in Black communities or from going to church or political rallies. Whether the songs are referred to as hymns, anthems, or spirituals, they represent the Black community uniting under one banner—a general understanding that the majority of Black people share. Not only were these songs sung in church, but also at school assemblies and almost always one can hear them during Black History Month celebrations.

A song is brought to life by the vocalist, and the voice that led the freedom movement's vision was Mahalia Jackson's. Jackson was a robust, sanctified singer who had a powerful voice and was committed to singing gospel music. She felt that gospel music was the sound of hope for the people. Jackson's spirit and drive to work in the civil rights movement alongside Martin Luther King and her resistance to being caught up in the fame of pop music culture helped her to have a strong connection with the Black churchgoing community. Jackson refused to sing anything but gospel because she felt that singing gospel provided a cure for what was wrong. When Jackson sang a song, you felt it down deep in your soul. She was called the Queen of Gospel Song, and some of her favorites include "A City Called Heaven," "I've Been 'Buked and I Been Scorned," "How I Got Over," and the song she sang for her martyred friend's funeral, "Take My Hand, Precious Lord" written by Thomas Dorsey. Dorsey is known for creating the concept of gospel—from the New Testament of the Holy Bible when he traveled from church to church, city to city, spreading the Good News. Dorsey, earlier in his life, was a blues pianist for Gertrude "Ma" Rainey (Mother of the Blues), then called *Georgia Tom* and now remembered as the *Father of Gospel.*

Questions to ponder:

- Why are these songs significant?
- How did these songs help to build communities?
- What is the *spirit* of these songs?

Chapter 4

Rhythm and Movement: Work Songs and the Blues

If you can walk you can dance, if you can talk you can sing.
—Zimbabwean Proverb

Spirituals and work songs are rooted in the slavery era and the West African societies from which most enslaved Africans were taken. These song styles provided cultural sustenance to African Americans in the midst of intense racial oppression. Folklorists like John and Alan Lomax recorded rural musicians from African Americans to Whites to Mexican Americans and began collecting this traditional southern music for the Library of Congress. The work of recording Black folk music probably started after 1865, although the songs that were documented were likely written in an earlier time. Without these recorders of history, most of the African story in antebellum America would not be known, for most of it was shared through oral forms of communication. Unfortunately, these songs were not collected and published until the 1930s and 1940s.

The rich culture of Black music usually comes out of religious worship or from work and labor. Black people sang in the fields as they worked during the week and in church on Sundays or any time they felt their spirits filled with hope and aspirations. This music was also the history of their pain and it was filled with metaphor and subtextual information. Historically, the Black song is a natural part of life's process for persons of African descent—an inherent part of the spirit. These blues and work songs inform, entertain, delight, and show that sadness, irony, nonsense, and the analysis of adversity and humor are but sides of the same coin (Belafonte, 2001).

The songs of labor and toil are explored in this section on rhythm and movement. The origins and connections to Africa in work songs and the blues will be discussed; how these musical inventions formed community; and why these memorable songs still have relevance today.

It was very common in Africa for men and women to sing as they worked, and this practice was a natural carryover for the enslaved Africans in North America. The fundamental law in Africa for a traditional form of communal work is to increase energy through music. These work songs have various names throughout Africa and the African diaspora: in Dahomey, they are called *dokpwe*; the Yoruba call them *egbe; coumbite* in Haiti; *troca dia* in Brazil; and *gayap* in Trinidad. The work becomes sort of a game or dance, invoking an excitement that becomes a driving force; the mind is distracted from the burdens of labor, singing becomes reality, and the work goes on automatic pilot and becomes subconscious (Jahn, 1961).

Slave masters have noted that enslaved Africans worked harder when they sang. A lead singer usually set the pace for the group. Those individuals with the strongest voices were auctioned at top prices. The utilitarian and artistic interrelationships of a steamboat work song were discussed by Wilson (1983), detailing the function of the task of chopping wood as an intrinsic part of the rhythm for the song. There is a presence of pendular thirds, call and response between voice and axe, and counter-rhythms sounded from the axe on the fourth beat in connection with weak beat accents against the strong beats of 4/4 meter. Wilson claims there is a synergistic relationship between work and song where the identity and use of the axe striking the wood become the drum rhythm (Wilson, 1983). Enslaved Africans were not singing because they were happy or content, they sang to *make* themselves happy and content, rather than to express their happiness through singing (Jahn, 1961).

In Africa and America, work songs were not just to keep people working but also to keep the workers organized and in sync with each other while farming or harvesting crops. Music enabled labors to get the work done in coordinated fashion. When Blacks are working together, especially for an important purpose, they sing as a group, and the songs tended to bind them as a community and make the work and less of an individualistic process.

Work was the main reason, and to some the only reason, why Africans were captured, enslaved, and brought to America (Evans, 2000). The slave system was a brutal, dehumanizing industry that enabled White southerners to thrive and prosper. To avoid the cruelties of their masters, mistresses, overseers, and drivers, they worked through this physical pain and emotional trauma. These enslaved Africans sang while they worked as a creative approach to living (Evans, 2000).

After slavery, Blacks still felt the brunt of Southern rage which indeed was a genuine and brutal undeclared war of revenge and retribution. Blacks were brutalized, their property was taken or destroyed, and Black men were charged with nonexistent crimes and illegally put in prison. In these prisons, Blacks were forced to become free laborers assigned to chain gangs in slavelike conditions. These men who were forced into chain gangs still made their time and labor less onerous through singing songs. Evans declared that African American work songs are the most poignant songs in the pantheon of Black music. Songs like "Early in the Mornin," "No More, My Lawd," and perhaps the most famous and long-lived of all African American ballads and work songs, "John Henry."

John Henry, Steel Driving Man

John Henry was a railroad man,
He worked from six till five, "Raise 'em up bul-
lies and let 'em drop down, I'll beat you to the
bottom or die."
John Henry said to his captain:

"You are nothing but a common man, Before that steam drill shall beat me down, I'll die with my hammer in my hand."
John Henry said to the Shakers:
"You must listen to my call, Before that steam drill shall beat me down, I'll jar these mountains till they fall."
John Henry's captain said to him:
"I believe these mountains are caving in." John Henry said to his captain: "Oh, Lord!" "That's my hammer you hear in the wind."
John Henry he said to his captain:
"Your money is getting mighty slim, When I hammer through this old mountain, Oh Captain will you walk in?"
John Henry's captain came to him
With fifty dollars in his hand, He laid his hand on his shoulder and said: "This belongs to a steel driving man."
John Henry was hammering on the right side,
The big steam drill on the left, Before that steam drill could beat him down, He hammered his fool self to death.
They carried John Henry to the mountains,
From his shoulder his hammer would ring, She caught on fire by a little blue blaze I believe these old mountains are caving in.
John Henry was lying on his death bed,
He turned over on his side, And these were the last words John Henry said: "Bring me a cool drink of water before I die."
John Henry had a little woman,
Her name was Pollie Ann, He hugged and kissed her just before he died, saying, "Pollie, do the very best you can."
John Henry's woman heard he was dead,

> She could not rest on her bed, She got up at midnight, caught that No. 4 train, "I am going where John Henry fell dead."
> They carried John Henry to that new burying ground
> His wife all dressed in blue, She laid her hand on John Henry's cold face, "John Henry I've been true to you."

Work songs are excellent primary sources in learning how illiterate (or rather, *so-called* illiterate) Black people from the time felt, from the spirit of their emotional outcries and pains, to the way the rhythm gave them the energy to want to dance, and to how their story was remembered and passed on and on through song. The concept of singing while you work was therapeutic and necessary for surviving during a time when there was little hope to live for. Songs like "John Henry, Steel Driving Man" and "Stagolee" helped people channel their egos, hopes, and desires into these immortal characters that they, too, will persevere.

Blues

The blues music is the culture of storytelling through music and the foundation of American popular music (Scorsese, 2003). Blues music is very similar in concept and style to the music of the griots in Mali, West Africa. Both styles use a string instrument to accompany their poetic narratives. Griots or *jalis (jelis)* were the historians for the Mandingo people. It was their job to remember the history of the people and share it through song and story. This shows how it is essential to know one's past to understand it. Once it is lost, you lose yourself (Scorsese, 2003).

> It is vital that people understand the roles and the power that the griot (known as *jali* and prefixed before the given family name) has been

endowed with since the beginning. One of the roles the griot in African society had before the Europeans came was maintaining a cultural and historical past with that of the present. He informed even to this day, men and women of the roles they must play in traditional African society. The griot was the oral historian and educator in any given society. The griot was well respected and was very close to kings—in fact, closer to the kings than the king's own wife.

The griot served as the king's confidant and personal advisor. The griot would interpret things, such as different facts, for the king. It was also the responsibility of the griot to make sure that the people received all the information about their ancestors—what the father, the grandparents, and their lineages had done and how they had done it. What the griot gave to African society in oral history, cultural information, and ancestral wisdom and knowledge is the key with which all people of African descent can progress and maintain a high level of understanding of their true heritage (Kouyate, 1989).

LeRoi Jones (Amiri Baraka) claimed in his historic social commentary text on the Negro experience, *The Blues People,* that the beginning of the blues is the beginning of the Americanized Negro (Jones, 1963). The work song had only a few English words, and the enslaved Africans on the plantation still had limited English language skills, but early blues which came after the Civil War moved toward more American-sounding lyrics. Jones further states that Negro work songs, which had origins in West Africa, are the immediate predecessor of the blues. As the work song began developing in America, much of the African ritual and cultural reference was removed. Nonetheless, the cultural connections of African American music, food, and sensibilities were still in tack with Africa. The blues may have become more American in its language but the spirit, rhythm, and story were still conceptually African.

The origin of the term *the blues* may have evolved from blue indigo which was used by many West African cultures in death or mourning. The color blue symbolized suffering. The enslaved Africans from West Africa, who sang of their suffering while working in the cotton fields, sang songs known as *the Blues*. South Carolina's major export crop in the eighteenth century was indigo. The musical connections between West and Central African music and the blues are the use of melisma and wavy nasal sound and the use of call and response. Moreover, the Akonting, a folk lute from the Jola people of Senegambia, is a clear predecessor to the American Negro banjo and has a similar playing style. It is probably the most critical link between African and African American music.

Rhythm has been the most apparent surviving remnant of African music, as well as the melodic similarities in singers' vocal interpretations. Vocal techniques, with tense, slightly hoarse-sounding sounds, seem to come directly from West African music traditions. In many West African languages, altering the pitch of the word can change the meaning of a word by changing the stress. Both pitch and timbre are used to produce changes in the meaning of words. The closest imitation of the human voice of any music is blues playing, according to Jones (1963).

The typical blues text has a stanza of three lines arranged:

A	A'	B
Statement	Statement	Resolution of
		repeated first
		two statements

(The statements are usually, but not always, rhymed.)

A is rarely an exact repeat but rather is altered by the addition of some exclamation in whatever slang is currently popular—such as *yeah, right, that's it, go head on.*

In West African music, the concept of the solo—a man or woman singing or playing by himself or herself—was relatively new. The

African concept of music and singing involved everyone and it was more communal. In blues singing, the separate events of appeal by the lead singer and answer by the chorus are consolidated into a single event by a single voice. A song in the community becomes a song before the community, since community now becomes a listener. The blues singer does not just express his personal experiences and transfer them to an audience, he becomes the spokesman for the experiences of the community (Jahn, 1961). Work songs, field hollers, and shouts were a cappella, but blues singing employed instruments to accompany the voice. This also brought a change for the vocalist who now conformed to an instrument's range and timbre. The choice instrument for blues singers was the guitar. The guitar strings can bend and shape the music like a vocalist would do. The guitar has its origin as well in West Africa and is from the banjo family, even traced to the akonting from Senegambia. The akonting was played by the hunters, mostly all men who bragged, told stories, and sang of their adventures and accomplishments.

In America, the early blues musicians were Black men and primarily farmers (cotton pickers), but the ones who felt they could survive set off on the road. The musician who best wore the title *Bluesman* was Robert Johnson. Johnson was a jook joint musician who looked like a bluesman. He always was well-dressed, preferably in a suit, shirt, and tie (including a hat, of course). Johnson was said to be crazy about women, loved to drink whiskey, and really knew how to play and sing the blues. He was born May 8, 1911, in Hazlehurst, Mississippi. (Johnson was not always a great blues player, and the legend suggests that Johnson sold his soul to the devil to become a great blues musician.)

The Mississippi Delta is where most historians claim that the blues began. However, it is hard to give one area more ownership to this claim than the other. Many enslaved Africans were taken to Mississippi during the Industrial Revolution when the large European textile manufactories were in high demand for raw cotton. The terrain and weather conditions were very similar to West Africa where many enslaved Africans were originally from. This work still was very difficult, and the temperature during cotton harvesting was unbearable in blazing conditions. Those musicians who were courageous (and maybe a little crazy) enough to escape this kind of work and avoid seizure by the chain gang patrols became troubadours—or in some aspects, griots. (Troubadours were musicians and poets from the medieval European minstrel period who traveled around the country as the preservers of the early secular song.)

Blues musicians, like both griots and troubadours, were traveling artists, storytellers, musicians, and entertainers, sharing what was going on in the south. Johnson became one of the first blues musicians that would develop his style of playing from several people he met in his travels. He enjoyed traveling around from town to town. People have confessed that Johnson would arrive in a new town, seek out the homeliest woman he could find, and charm her with his words, handsome looks, and guitar picking so that he would have a place to stay while in town. To some, he was a typical musician—one that messed around, drank booze (drugs), gambled, and did not want to settle down. Robert Johnson was considered the greatest blues musician who ever lived. His high tenor voice remains one of the most powerful cries found in the human voice. His vast repertoire of songs has had a large effect on understanding the time in which he lived. His music in general has helped to develop American popular music culture which in turn has formed a large community of people around the world.

One of Robert Johnson's notable works that is still played, listened to, and studied is "Terraplane Blues"—Johnson's first hit song which uses his woman allowing someone to drive his Terraplane car while he was out of town as sexual metaphor. "Hellhound on My Trail," on the other hand, was about escaping from slavery or the prison gang.

> I got to keep moving, blues falling down like hail,
> And the day keeps on remindin' me, there's a
> hellhound on my trail.
> If today was Christmas eve, And tomorrow was
> Christmas day;
> If all I would need is my little sweet rider just to
> pass the time away.
> You sprinkled hot foot powder, mmm, around
> my door.

It keeps me with ramblin' mind rider;
Every old place I go,
I can tell the wind is risin', the leaves tremblin'
    on the tree.
All I need is my little sweet woman to keep my
    company. (Robert Johnson, 1937).

"Crossroad Blues" has generated the myth about Johnson going down to the crossroads to sell his soul to the devil in order to play guitar the way he did. Its lyrics do strongly resemble the Yoruba deity, Esu-Elegba, who is considered as the gatekeeper and trickster god: an essentially protective spirit who serves as a messenger between heaven and earth. Esu-Elegba requires constant appeasement in order to carry out his functions of transmitting sacrifices and divining the future (Bhutia, 2015).

I went to the crossroad, fell down on my knees
I went to the crossroad, fell down on my knees
Asked the Lord above
'Have mercy now, save poor Bob, if you please'

Yeoo, standin' at the crossroad, tried to flag a ride
Ooo, eeee, I tried to flag a ride
Didn't nobody seem to know me, babe, every-
    body pass me by

Standin' at the crossroad, baby, risin' sun goin' down
Standin' at the crossroad, baby, eee, eee, risin' sun
    goin' down
I believe to my soul, now, poor Bob is sinkin' down

And I went to the crossroad, mama, I looked east
    and west
I went to the crossroad, baby, I looked east and west
Lord, I didn't have no sweet woman
Oh well, babe, in my distress. (Robert Johnson, 1936)

If Robert Johnson is depicted as a bluesman, then Bessie Smith was the Empress of the Blues. Ma Rainey, her elder, was the true prototype of a woman blues singer in the South. However, it was Bessie Smith who took the blues to the big southern cities and up north. Her story and life seem to be well depicted in the song, "Nobody Knows You When You Are Down and Out." Jimmy Cox composed the song in 1923, and Smith's recording of it became popular.

> Once I lived the life of a millionaire,
> Spent all my money, I just did not care.
> Took all my friends out for a good time,
> Bought bootleg whisky, champagne and wine.
>
> Then I began to fall so low,
> Lost all my good friends, I did not have nowhere
>   to go.
> I get my hands on a dollar again, I'm gonna hang
>   on to it till that eagle grins.
>
> [chorus]
>
> 'Cause no, no, nobody knows you When you're
>   down and out.
> In your pocket, not one penny, And as for friends,
>   you don't have any.
>
> When you finally get back up on your feet again,
>   Everybody wants to be your old long-lost
>   friend. Said it's mighty strange, without a
>   doubt,
> Nobody knows you when you're down and out.
>   (Jimmy Cox, 1923)

It is still the song that most people associate Bessie Smith with. After she recorded it in 1929, the stock market crashed, and the song seemed like a premonition of what was to come. Blues vocalists were not recorded until 1920. Mamie Smith was the first blues singer to record in 1920, "Crazy Blues." Mamie Smith was not generally viewed as a blues singer. She was a vaudeville or cabaret singer, dancer, pianist, and actress who the recording industry felt was comfortable, safe not to start a major race riot. Bessie Smith recorded on race records where most Blacks recorded, but Mamie Smith recorded with Okeh Records. "Crazy Blues" was a best seller, with over a million copies sold in the first year.

The female blues singers were at the junction and transition from the blues to jazz. They transformed the rural blues into sophisticated city dance music. The bands that accompanied the blues singers tended to be made up of jazz musicians. Thus, the jazz age has begun!

In 1912, the first blues song published was by William Christopher Handy, "Memphis Blues." Handy is known as the Father of the Blues because he was the first to compose and publish a large volume of blues songs. "Memphis Blues" was originally titled "Mister Crump" because Handy was inspired in 1909 to create a song to help a local politician, E.H. Crump, become mayor. Handy was born on November 16, 1873, in Florence, Alabama, the son and grandson of Methodist ministers. Although his father did not want him to become a musician, Handy was drawn to the laborers singing during visits to his grandfather's farm and was always eager to learn more about music. Handy was fortunate to have a teacher at his Negro public school, Y. A. Wallace, who was from Fisk University. Wallace drilled the students with singing the sol-fa system until they could perform unaccompanied choruses from the great European classical composers—Wagner, Verdi, and Bizet. Handy was able to study with Mr. Wallace for eleven years. During Handy's formative years as a musician, he became the cornet soloist, eventually bandmaster and orchestra leader of the famous Mahara's Colored Minstrels from 1896 to 1903. This was a typical way for most Negro musicians to make a living during this period. The Mahara's band played in Oakland, California, in 1897. Handy remembers playing a coronet solo, "Mia," by Hartmann, and receiving applause from the box seats where Whites sat, but missing from the gallery where most Blacks gathered. Handy recalls the next night playing the hit song, "Georgia Camp Meeting," to which he welcomed undivided applause (Niles, 1926).

Handy, in the summer of 1912, published a thousand copies of "Memphis Blues" to try selling them on the music counter at Bry's Department Store where a White man, L.Z. Phillips, who volunteered to help Handy, was employed. The music department concessionaire at Bry's was Theron C. Bennett, a Denver publisher who came to Memphis to assist as the selling agent for this musical document. After a week or so, Bennett convinced Handy that because the composition was too difficult, no one was buying it and a thousand copies were still on the store shelf. Bennett offered to take a gamble and a huge risk paying fifty dollars for the copyright, royalty-free. Handy, feeling discouraged, took Bennett up on his offer. Bennett ordered ten thousand more copies of the song. He reported that the first thousand copies of "Memphis Blues" sold out in three days. In fact, he originally had two thousand copies made, not a thousand, and was able to trick Handy into selling the copyright (Niles, 1926).

Luckily, Handy did not sit around mourning the loss of his hit song but set about producing a new one. That is what he did in 1914 when "St. Louis Blues" was published.

W.C. Handy was a true artist, troubadour, and musical scholar. He is also credited with introducing the habanera or tango rhythm, which musically noted as a dotted quarter, an eighth, and two-quarter notes, which Handy uses in the accompanying bass patterns of his blues. This pattern was implied in "Memphis Blues" and made more explicit in "St. Louis Blues." Bessie Smith recorded the vocals for "St. Louis Blues" in 1925 which became a major hit for her, as well. William Christopher Handy's work will continue to live on as the foundation for all American music which has its roots in the blues, and he will be remembered as the Father of the Blues.

Although some would argue that Handy was not even a blues musician, in fact most of the bands in the cities that backed blues singers were considered more as jazz musicians. The fills that instrumentalists made in the pauses between the blues vocalist's singing became to be called *the jazz*. The "Memphis Blues" breaks were probably not the first breaks ever played, but Handy and his band exploited this technique which later became a jazz standard feature (Niles, 1926). Every time I hear "St. Louis Blues," I will give a salute to W. C. Handy for his awareness to document this great American art form called the Blues, especially being that he was a Black man.

> I hate to see de evenin' sun go down,
> Hate to see de evenin' sun go down
> 'Cause ma baby, he done lef' dis town.
> Feelin' tomorrow like I feel today,
> Feel tomorrow like I feel today,
> I'll pack my trunk, make ma git away.
> Saint Louis woman wid her diamon' rings
> Pulls dat man 'roun' by her apron strings.
> 'Twant for powder an' for store-bought hair,
> De man ah love would not gone nowhere, nowhere.
> Got de Saint Louis Blues jes as blue as ah can be.
> That man got a heart lak a rock cast in the sea.
>
> Or else he wouldn't have gone so far from me.
> > Doggone it!
> I loves day man lak a schoolboy loves his pie,
> Lak a Kentucky Col'nel loves his mint an' rye.
> I'll love ma baby till the day ah die.
>
> Been to de gypsy to get ma fortune tole,
> To de gypsy, done got ma fortune tole,
> Cause I'm most wile 'bout ma Jelly Roll.
> Gypsy done tole me, "Don't you wear no black."
> Yes, she done told me, "Don't you wear no black.

That man got a heart lak a rock cast in the sea.
Or else he wouldn't have gone so far from me.
    Doggone it!
I loves day man lak a schoolboy loves his pie,
Lak a Kentucky Colonel loves his mint an' rye.
I'll love ma baby till the day I die.

You ought to see dat stovepipe brown of mine,
Lak he owns de Dimon' Joseph line,
He'd make a cross-eyed o'man go stone blin'.
Blacker than midnight, teeth lak flags of truce,
Blackest man in de whole of Saint Louis,
Blacker de berry, sweeter am de juice.
About a crap game, he knows a pow'ful lot,
But when worktime comes, he's on de dot.
Gwine to ask him for a cold ten-spot,
What it takes to git it, he's cert'nly got.

Got de Saint Louis Blues jes as blue as ah can be.
Dat man got a heart lak a rock cast in the sea.
Or else he wouldn't have gone so far from me.
    Doggone it!
I loves day man lak a schoolboy loves his pie,
Lak a Kentucky Col'nel loves his mint an' rye.
I'll love ma baby till the day ah die.

A black-headed gal makes a freight train jump
    the track, said a black-headed
Gal makes a freight train jump the track,
But a long tall gal makes a preacher ball the jack.

Lawd, a blonde-headed woman makes a good
    man leave the town, I said
Blonde-headed woman makes a good man leave
    the town,
But a red-headed woman makes a boy slap his
    papa down.

Oh, ashes to ashes and dust to dust, I said ashes
    to ashes and dust to dust,
If my blues don't get you, my jazzing must. (W.C.
    Handy, 1914)

Chapter 5

The Story in Art And Song: Jazz and Soul Music

When the music changes, so does the dance.
—Nigerian Proverb

*B*lues provided musicians with an artistic framework to build and develop specific styles and new musical idioms. The female blues vocalist articulated a personal presence in the male-dominated industry of jazz. These cabaret singers, now given the title of jazz vocalist, transformed the blues into forms of jazz, women such as Dinah Washington, Billie Holiday, and Nina Simone. Jazz music is considered art music or classical music that is to be studied. It differs from work songs and blues, even those that are figured to be more sophisticated and intellectual.

Southern trees bear strange fruit
Blood on the leaves and blood at the root
Black bodies swinging in the southern breeze
Strange fruit hanging from the poplar trees
Pastoral scene of the gallant south
The bulging eyes and the twisted mouth
Scent of magnolias, sweet and fresh
Then the sudden smell of burning flesh
Here is fruit for the crows to pluck

> For the rain to gather, for the wind to suck
> For the sun to rot, for the trees to drop
> Here is a strange and bitter crop. (Abel Meeropol,
> 1937)

One of the greatest jazz songs, "Strange Fruit" recorded by Billie Holiday in 1939, was about American racism and particularly the lynching of African Americans. Holiday's version of this song has been inducted into the Grammy Hall of Fame and is on the list of Songs of the Century, a list compiled by the Recording Industry of America and the Endowment of the Arts. A Jewish schoolteacher and member of the Communist Party, Abel Meeropol, wrote this song. He was married to a Black vocalist, Laura Duncan, who sang the song in Madison Square Garden (Margolick, 2001). The song is reliable as a vivid description of the cruelties placed mainly on Black men—a protest of the highest order that helped to bring these atrocities to a stop. If music can be used to change how people feel and to bring them strength and dignity, then a song becomes a part of the community.

In discussing the various movements that African Americans have inspired through history, such as the Harlem Renaissance, civil rights, and the Black Power movement, it is interesting to denote what was the music of choice of these movements and how the songs were used to build community. The Harlem Renaissance, which took place around the 1920s, used spirituals as the music of choice or maybe a classically arranged jazz suite, such as Ellington's "Sacred Suite." Even though this period was marked as the Jazz Age, most of the Black intellectual scholars then felt jazz was still popular music, not sophisticated or classy enough for the Negro Renaissance. The civil rights movement used freedom songs, various renditions of spirituals and folk songs, and changed lyrics to have the message of the time heard and felt. These freedom songs seemed to reach the moral and emotional consciousness of White Americans, as the *spirit* of the music touched them. Jazz music progressed from the 1920s to sixties, and a new group of *modernists* emerged. These were not typical swing players. Although Louis Armstrong and Duke Ellington are the royal family elders of the jazz scene, it was artists like Dizzy, Bird, Monk, Trane, and Miles that made jazz Black nationalist music for the Black Power movement.

The story of jazz cannot be accurately told without including Louis Armstrong, or Pops as he is more affectionately known. Armstrong, born and raised in New Orleans, first played coronet but eventually became the number one soloist and jazzman of all times, according to most jazz historians. His ability to sing the blues and improvise variations on melodies is still marveled at today. Armstrong's rendition of "What a Wonderful World" is still popular and "West End Blues" has to be the greatest musical solo on an introduction to a song ever made (according to my good friend and colleague, Dr. Imara). His contemporary, Edward Kennedy "Duke" Ellington, was recognized as a great American composer, and "Take the A Train" is a personal favorite. I will not spend much time discussing these great jazz artists or even others such as Miles Davis (considered by most jazz surveys to be the top jazz artist of all time due to his album *Kind of Blue* selling more copies than any other jazz record), since this book's focus is on vocal songs and how they have unified and moved the community—in spirit, rhythm, and story.

There are various jazz styles. New Orleans was known as the origin place of jazz music, but like the blues, it is hard for one place to take credit. Jazz has origins in West Africa where the term *dinza* might have been creolized in New Orleans and through Black America into *jizz* and *jism* which is explained by Robert Ferris Thompson:

"Ki-Kongo words and concepts influenced black English, especially the lexicons of jazz and the blues, as well as lovemaking and herbalism" (1984). Etymologists have described many a Ki-Kong derived word as *origin unknown*. Thompson further illustrates that "The word *jazz* probably creolized Ki-Kongo and it is similar in sound and original meaning to *jizz*, the American vernacular for semen. Moreover, *jizz*, suggestive of vitality, appears to derive from the Ki-Kongo verb *dinza,* to discharge one's semen, to come" (Thompson, 1984). Although most jazz historians claim New Orleans as the birthplace of Jazz in America, the first jazz clubs may have been in San Francisco, California. San Francisco, during the

World War I and postwar period, had a rich social and cultural history where leading San Franciscans frequented certain Negro night spots. There were clubs like Purcell, the Jupiter, and the Olympia which hosted dozens of African American musicians, including the New Orleans pianist legend Jelly Roll Morton who, by some regard, was a founding father of jazz due to his interpretation of "Maple Leaf Rag" by Scott Joplin, which helped to transform ragtime to early jazz. The first printed use of the word *jazz* in relationship with syncopated nonclassical music happened in 1913 found in an article written by "Scoop" Gleason in a San Francisco Call-Bulletin newspaper (Pepin, Elizabeth, 2001).

Jazz saxophonist John Coltrane's instrumental "Alabama," inspired by the Sixteenth Street Baptist Church bombing that killed four black girls in Birmingham in September 1963, expressed a depth of grief and rage that no lyric could possibly intensify. The whole of the avant-garde or free jazz movement that claimed Coltrane, along with other prodigiously gifted musicians such as Cecil Taylor, Albert Ayler, Ornette Coleman, and Pharoah Sanders (The Creator has a Master Plan) as major influences, was predicated on a self-conscious rejection of Western—interpreted as White—notions of musical correctness. Many of these musicians hoped to escape what they saw as the tyranny of White cultural expectations and standards by substituting a Black aesthetic which would give precedence to a different uniquely African American standard of musical excellence. As such, their musical experimentation represented a more radical expression of the kind of discontent with the racial status quo that inspired the civil rights struggle, coupled with a determination to secure respect for distinctively African American values that would become a hallmark of the Black Power era in the late 1960s and early 1970s. The accomplishments of these musicians help to illustrate the important point that the political and social significance of all black music, be it jazz, soul, or the freedom songs, was often encoded in its rhythms, timbres, harmonies, and melodies (Ward, 2012).

The jazz music that gets the most attention is the instrumental style which is also how this writer became connected and mesmerized by the power of jazz. When my brother, who just returned home for the summer from his freshman year in college, played John Coltrane's version of "My Favorite Things," I felt a strong emotional yearning for this music called jazz for the first time. Coltrane's tenor saxophone playing held me glued to the speaker, wondering what he was saying in the music. What also impressed me was that on the cover of one of his albums was a map of Africa. With tunes like "Afro Blue," I felt a sense of energy coming through me as I was being transformed. Then after hearing "A Love Supreme," I knew what Trane, as most of my jazz musician buddies referred to Coltrane, was dedicated to producing music that had spirit, rhythm, and story. This became my favorite music to listen to and the style of jazz that I wanted to play. The piano players—Thelonious Monk and McCoy Tyner—became my new teachers.

The jazz music played on the few jazz radio programs still around is primarily instrumental, and when they play vocal jazz, it is often done by either a White singer or written by a White composer. White lyricists wrote the majority of jazz standards, Except for the jazz style that is viewed as the most complex—bebop, where there were strong Black lyricist/poets. Bebop was the main jazz sound of the 1940s through 1960s. Luckily, there were some great Black poets and lyricists that prevailed—the likes of Eddie Jefferson (1918–1979), Jon Hendrix (b. 1921), and Oscar Brown Jr. (1926–2005) during this style period. They took the lively and rhythmic jazz tunes and solos of Trane, Bird, Monk, and Miles and put words to them by interpreting the story of jazz.

Soul Music and its Influence on the Black Power Movement

Stevie Wonder is indeed a leader in advocating for the community through song. He was one of the leaders of soul music (sixties to eighties) which was initially a term used to describe the new sound of jazz in the 1960s with artists like Betty Carter and Stanley Turrentine. Wonder expressed a cultural nationalism and introduced a political element to popular music (Ramsey, 2003). Wonder ("Living for the City"), along with Marvin Gaye ("What's Going On"), Gil Scott-Heron ("Winter in America"), and Donny Hathaway ("The Ghetto"), revolutionized the music scene in the seventies. But the song used as a standard for the sixties is "A Change is Gonna Come" by Sam Cooke, a gospel singer who crossed over to secular music and became one of the best soul singers until his tragic death at a young age. This song was used in the memorial of El Hajj Malik El Shabazz (Malcolm X). The message was that the people had had enough and the peaceful demonstrations of the civil rights movement were over. It was time to mobilize and attack.

"A Change is Gonna Come" was released as a single eleven days after Sam Cooke died from gunshots in a South Central Los Angeles motel in December 1964. Cooke was born in the heart of the Mississippi Delta but raised in the Chicago Bronzeville area. His father, Charles Cook, was a socially conservative preacher in the Holiness Church. Sam later changed the spelling of his last name after he moved from sacred to secular music. Cooke first became popular in the Soul Stirrers, a popular gospel quartet, but wanted to crossover to pop music and make more money. Cooke's appeal was his unconventional style of singing. The top male gospel singers of the day were Ira Tucker of the Dixie Hummingbirds, Clarence Fountain of the Five Blind Boys of Alabama, and Claude Jeter of the Swain Silvertones, and their voices were raw and powerful. However, Cooke's sound was not the traditional moan but a softer, higher tone that embellished the melody and gave his listeners a sense of promise and hope, not the redemptive vision most gospel singers were projecting. Cooke had recorded a series of successful hits from "Cupid," "Wonderful World," and "You Send Me" before releasing "A Change is Gonna Come" which was considered his best composition and became an anthem for the civil rights and Black Power movements. Werner, in his book *A Change is Gonna Come*, states that this "song expresses the soul of the freedom movement as clearly and powerfully as King's 'Letter from the Birmingham Jail'" (Weiner, 1999, p. 33). The song begins with the sound of French horns swelling over the strings and symphony, with the tympani drums laying the beat. Cooke's somewhat autobiographical sketch in the song states that he was born by a river in a tent and life has been hard, but he knows from his faith roots that a change will come:

> I was born by the river in a little tent
> Oh and just like the river I've been running ever
>   since
> It's been a long, a long time coming
> But I know a change gonna come, oh yes it will
> It's been too hard living but I'm afraid to die
> 'Cause I don't know what's up there beyond the sky
> It's been a long, a long time coming
> But I know a change gonna come, oh yes it will
>
> I go to the movie and I go downtown
> Somebody keep telling me, 'Don't hang around'
> It's been a long, a long time coming
> But I know a change gonna come, oh yes it will
>
> Then I go to my brother
> And I say, 'Brother, help me, please'
> But he winds up knockin' me
> Back down on my knees
> Oh there been times that I thought I couldn't last
>   for long
> But now I think I'm able to carry on
> It's been a long, a long time coming
> But I know a change gonna come. (Sam Cooke,
>   1964)

Also important to the Black Power movement was James Brown's revolutionary song, "Say It Loud, I'm Black and Proud." From an old African American's perspective, the song moves from self-rejection to a new anthem and cry: I'm Black and I'm proud! This song is considered a *funk* song, but a part of soul as well. Funk was a genre of Black music developed in the late 1960s as a more danceable groove than the soul music. Brown's song, "Say it

Loud…" was written in 1968, peaked on Billboards Top 100 songs at number ten, and became the unofficial song anthem of the Black Power movement.

> Look a'here, some people say we got a lot of malice
> Some say it's a lotta nerve
> I say we won't quit moving
> 'Til we get what we deserve
>
> We've been 'buked and we've been scorned
> We've been treated bad, talked about
> As just as sure as you're born
> But just as sure as it take
> Two eyes to make a pair, huh
> Brother, we can't quit until we get our share
>
> [*Chorus*]
>
> Say it loud,
> I'm black and I'm proud
> Say it loud,
> I'm black and I'm proud, one more time
> Say it loud,
> I'm black and I'm proud, huh
>
> I've worked on jobs with my feet and my hands
> But all the work I did was for the other man
> And now we demands a chance
> To do things for ourselves
> we tired of beating our heads against the wall
> And working for someone else
>
> [*Chorus*]
>
> One thing more I got to say right here
> Now, we're people like the birds and the bees

We rather die on our feet,
Than keep living on our knees. (James Brown
and Pee Wee Ellis, 1968)

The story of the Black revolution, or Black Power movement, in America was told in songs. Rickey Vincent (2013) articulates this thought very well in his new book *Party Music* by stating that "every song tells a story," and the stories told in songs from the 1960s were dramatic and life-changing. This period involved a radical change in America's mainstream discourse. Blacks wanted to overturn the social order of the White supremacist caste system that was plaguing America's urban communities. Soul music was the new popular Black sound, and the great soul singers were dominating the market—James Brown, Aretha Franklin, Sam Cooke, Otis Redding, and others—whose music was invoking more than just dance moves. Soul music meant various things for Black people, but mainly it was a pride thing for anything to be called soul, whether it was food, music, or a person—soul brother or soul sister referred to Black people.

James Brown, to some, was an unlikely choice to become an advocate for the Black Power movement. One, Brown was making too much money; and two, he had strong ties to the Republican Party and was friends with President Nixon. Many Black nationalist and progressive leaders, such as the Black Panthers, referred to Brown as an Uncle Tom, meaning he cared more for White people than he did his own. By the summer of 1968, Blacks were in an uproar and were demanding change, even if it meant violence. King was dead and James Brown was under fire to release a song with a political message. On August 7, 1968, Brown recorded "Say it Loud, I'm Black and Proud" at the Vox studio on Melrose Street in Los Angeles (Vincent, 2013).

Brown's song became a turning point in Black popular culture and in the music particularly. No Black music up to that point was able to reflect the bitterness of Black people toward Whites in such a popular fashion. Other musical genres like spirituals, blues, and even jazz never had the popularity that soul music had, and tunes such as "Strange Fruit" by Billie Holiday in 1938 and Coltrane's "Alabama" in 1963 moved people's consciousness but were never given the popularity that "Say it Loud..." had. Even the term *Black* was now the new preferred nomenclature for African Americans. It seems that Africans in America have been given more names than most any other group of people—names from Slave, African, Bantu, Nigga, Gullah, Geechee, Negro, Colored, Race Man, Black, Soul Man, Afro-American, and now presently, African American (without the hyphen). By 1970, most African Americans wanted to be called Black and being Negro was no longer acceptable, especially for the youth. The term Black gave people a sense of empowerment and liberation. "Say it Loud..." gave the Black community pride and purpose while capturing the soul aesthetic. Although "Say it Loud..." led to a downturn of Brown's career, especially with his White fans, it helped to spark a radicalism in Black people. After the release of Brown's hit song, there were songs of pride and Black anthems from many other popular Black acts: Temptations with "Message from a Black Man," the Impressions with "Choice of Colors," and Sly and Family Stone's "Don't Call Me Nigger, Whitey." This song also invigorated the writers, poets, and political artists of the day, like the great political novelist and jazz poet Gil Scott-Heron (Vincent, 2013).

The Life and Legacy of Gil Scott-Heron

Growing up in the sixties in the East Bay Area, particularly in Parchester Village in Richmond, California, was an interesting, exciting, and creative experience. As a young person, I was open to my surroundings and inspired by the *music of change*, or as some would call it, *revolutionary* music. It was during the time that big afros and dashikis were in fashion. In my neighborhood, Black Muslims sold their newspapers door to door; the Black Panthers were present and had one of their major headquarters in our village. Men wore black leather jackets and saluted you with a tightened black fist to represent power. You were greeted with expressions like "Black is beautiful" and "Power to the people." It was time of respect for the elders; you addressed them with *sir* or *ma'am* as you spoke to them. Folks were poor but proud and never let you see them begging or giving up.

This was the time of the Black Power movement. Malcolm X stood as the rightful leader of this revolutionary change. The Bay Area was a key area of influence during these times. Merritt College in Oakland started a Black studies course which led to San Francisco State University implementing a Black studies department in 1968. Young African Americans were intrigued by the rhetoric and protest demands of our leaders and especially moved by the music. Aretha Franklin was belting out songs like "Respect," and Curtis Mayfield was letting us know that it was time to prepare ourselves for change.

> People get ready, there's a train a comin'
> You don't need no baggage, you just get on board
> All you need is faith to hear the diesels hummin'
> Don't need no ticket, you just thank the Lord.
> (Curtis Mayfield, 1964)

The poets were leading the way with their strong literary portrayals of the abuse of the Amerikkkan capitalist system, keeping people of color down, poor, hungry, confused, and misinformed. Amiri Baraka was another major contributor to the movement with his radical poetry, Black Art:

> Poems are bullshit unless they are
> teeth or trees or lemons piled
> on a step. Or black ladies dying
> of men leaving nickel hearts
> beating them down. Fuck poems
> and they are useful, wd they shoot
> come at you, love what you are,
> breathe like wrestlers, or shudder
> strangely after pissing. We want live
> words of the hip world live flesh and
> coursing blood. Hearts Brains
> Souls splintering fire. We want poems

> like fists beating niggers out of Jocks
> or dagger poems in the slimy bellies
> of the owner-jews. Black poems to
> smear on girdlemamma mulatto bitches
> whose brains are red jelly stuck
> between 'lizabeth taylor's toes. Stinking
> Whores! we want 'poems that kill.'
> Assassin poems, Poems that shoot guns. (Amiri
> Baraka, 1965)

Baraka is a brilliant poet who presents his words with such force and passion that you are left with a sense of the pain that he describes and delivers with such emotion. He is letting us know that a poem has to be more than words. It must call the people to action.

By the start of the seventies, I was thirteen. I felt so special to now call myself a teenager. I experimented with alcohol and marijuana during this age, since I had an older brother five years my elder who was engaged in that lifestyle at the time—girls, clothes, drugs, and the music. He would decorate our room with psychedelic posters of his favorite artists: Jimi Hendrix, Santana, Sly and the Family Stone, and others. But what caught my attention the most was the music that was played, especially the lyrics from artists like The Last Poets and Gil Scott-Heron. At this point in my life, I began to have aspirations of becoming a musician. I bought my first keyboard—a Fender Rhodes electric piano. My father helped me to set up monthly payments and used the money that I made working cleaning up the church on Saturdays and cutting lawns in the neighborhood as reimbursement. All of my favorite musicians also played the Fender Rhodes: Stevie Wonder, Donny Hathaway, Ramsey Lewis, and especially Gil Scott-Heron. I would try to imitate these artists and incorporate their songs in my repertoire. I began to play in a local band and perform for money. This made me more aware of the music that was played around me, either from the local radio stations or from my brother and his record collections. I was truly intrigued by these album covers and the song titles. One group that stood out the most was The Last Poets. Song titles like "Run, Nigger," "Niggers

Are Scared of Revolution," and "When the Revolution Comes" were insightful, somewhat scary, and truly grown folks' themes of the times. These were poets stating powerful phrases with a shocking and resonating vocabulary of profanity, with drums beating with passionately in the background. The drums reminded me of the conga drums that the Black Panthers would play in my village. I recall that when they were having a meeting, there would be a few men sitting in front of the office building playing their drums. I was told later if the police were coming, the drums would stop to signal the brothers inside that something was wrong. These drums started to have a strong meaning in the community.

As curious as I was about The Last Poets, I did not really understand their messages. Then I discovered Gil Scott-Heron. His music and lyrics gelled for me and opened my eyes to the message in the music. Scott-Heron once stated that he was inspired to start a group after watching a performance of The Last Poets in 1969. It seemed like I was going through a transformation, discovering myself and the music in me. Gil Scott-Heron was known as an American soul and jazz poet who authored his first novel at nineteen entitled *The Vulture*. Gil's charisma, smooth delivery, and soulful singing style made his music popular and significant to the messages of the day. He sang songs about alcohol abuse ("The Bottle"), how racism and negativity were affecting Black and people of color ("Winter in America"), and one of my favorites: "The Revolution Will Not Be Televised."

> You will not be able to stay home, brother.
> You will not be able to plug in, turn on and drop
>   out.
> You will not be able to lose yourself on skag and
>   skip,
> Skip out for beer during commercials
> Because the revolution will not be televised.
>
> The revolution will not be televised.

The revolution will not be brought to you by Xerox
In 4 parts without commercial interruption.
The revolution will not show you pictures of Nixon
Blowing a bugle and leading a charge by John
     Mitchell,
General Abrams and Spiro Agnew to eat
Hog maws confiscated from a Harlem sanctuary.

The revolution will not be televised.

The revolution will be brought to you by the
     Schaefer Award Theatre and
will not star Natalie Wood and Steve McQueen
     or Bullwinkle and Julia.
The revolution will not give your mouth sex appeal.
The revolution will not get rid of the nubs.
The revolution will not make you look five pounds
Thinner, because The revolution will not be tele-
     vised, Brother.

There will be no pictures of you and Willie Mays
Pushing that cart down the block on the dead run,
Or trying to slide that color television into a sto-
     len ambulance.
NBC will not predict the winner at 8:32or the
     count from 29 districts.

The revolution will not be televised.

There will be no pictures of pigs shooting down
Brothers in the instant replay.
There will be no pictures of young being
Run out of Harlem on a rail with a brand new
     process
There will be no slow motion or still life of

Roy Wilkens strolling through Watts in a red,
    black and
Green liberation jumpsuit that he had been saving
For just the right occasion
Green Acres, The Beverly Hillbillies, and
Hooterville Junction will no longer be so damned
    relevant,
and Women will not care if Dick finally gets
    down with
Jane on Search for Tomorrow because Black people
will be in the street looking for a brighter day.

The revolution will not be televised.

There will be no highlights on the eleven o'clock
    News
and no pictures of hairy armed women Liberationists
    and
Jackie Onassis blowing her nose.
The theme song will not be written by Jim Webb,
    Francis Scott Key,
nor sung by Glen Campbell, Tom Jones, Johnny
    Cash,
Englebert Humperdink, or the Rare Earth.

The revolution will not be televised

The revolution will not be right back after a message
About a white tornado, white lightning, or white
    people.
You will not have to worry about a germ on your
    Bedroom,
a tiger in your tank, or the giant in your toilet bowl.
The revolution will not go better with Coke.
The revolution will not fight the germs that cause
    bad breath.

The revolution WILL put you in the driver's seat.
The revolution will not be televised,

WILL not be televised, WILL NOT BE
    TELEVISED.

The revolution will be no re-run brothers;
The revolution will be live.

You will not be able to stay home, brother.
You will not be able to plug in, turn on and drop
    out.
You will not be able to lose yourself on skag and skip,
Skip out for beer during commercials
Because the revolution will not be televised.

The revolution will not be televised…

There will be no pictures of pigs shooting down
Brothers in the instant replay.
There will be no pictures of young being
Run out of Harlem on a rail with a brand new
    process
There will be no slow motion or still life of
Roy Wilkens strolling through Watts in a red,
    black and
Green liberation jumpsuit that he had been saving
For just the right occasion
Green Acres, The Beverly Hillbillies, and
Hooterville Junction will no longer be so damned
    relevant,
and Women will not care if Dick finally gets down
    with
Jane on Search for Tomorrow because Black people
will be in the street looking for a brighter day.

The revolution will not be televised…

The revolution will not be right back after a message
About a white tornado, white lightning, or white
        people.
You will not have to worry about a germ on your
        Bedroom,
a tiger in your tank, or the giant in your toilet
        bowl.
The revolution will not go better with Coke.
The revolution will not fight the germs that cause
        bad breath.
The revolution *will* put you in the driver's seat.
The revolution will not be televised,

Will not be televised, *will not be televised.*
The revolution will be no re-run brothers;
The revolution will be live. (Gil Scott-Heron, 1970)

It seems that Gil Scott-Heron is saying in the song that people want changes but do not want to do anything to make those changes, so if you want *revolution*, you cannot sit and wait for it to come on your television set. This song made a strong impact on my life and journey as a musician and educator.

Amiri Baraka's book, *Blues People*, is an interesting way to depict Black people in America. We are the story of the blues, but what is so appealing about the blues is it makes you stronger through the healing tonic of its story. Gil Scott-Heron referred to himself as a bluesologist. He wanted the people to be transformed by his messages and move them to action.

In my life, I have been fortunate to travel around the world and play music and work in the field of education. I am a graduate of San Francisco State University with bachelor's degrees in music and Black studies, a master's in creative arts, and a doctorate in educational leadership. I am a community college full-time professor. I have met and performed on the same stage with many of my idols, such as

The Last Poets and Gil Scott-Heron. I am still moved and inspired by the legacy of their music, lyrics, and poetry. I am blessed with having lived in a period in which revolutionary music was popular and played on local radio stations, and so thankful that I am able to pass on these same influences and messages to students, colleagues, friends, and family.

Stevie Wonder: Songwriter and Humanitarian

Stevie Wonder, more than any other musician and songwriter, has had an enormous impact on this writer. His amazing music touches the inner soul, moves the rhythmic pulse, and makes us conscious of what is going on. Wonder embodies how Black musicians, icons, and songwriters should model themselves as responsible caregivers to help in the efforts of community building, helping people to be mindful, aware, conscious, and excited to be human. Wonder was born in 1950 in Saginaw, Michigan, and his family later moved to Detroit where he grew up. After being born six weeks premature, he developed an eye disease—retinopathy of prematurity—and became blind. Through his amazing use of hearing, becoming a musical genius and political and cultural consciousness advocate, Wonder has helped the world see a better place. I have learned how to play more Stevie Wonder songs than any other songwriter. I have so many favorites, but the songs that have had an impact on my life are ones in which he educates on the history of Black people and the issues faced. Songs like "Black Man" and "Bamboozled" are oral history lessons.

Another critical song was Stevie Wonder's "Living for the City"—notice the strong messages, sort of a community narrative of being a Black man in the inner city:

> A boy is born in hard time Mississippi
> Surrounded by four walls that ain't so pretty
> His parents give him love and affection
> To keep him strong moving in the right direction

Chorus: Living just enough, just enough for the
     city…ee ha!
His hair is long, his feet are hard and gritty
He spends his life walking the streets of New
     York City
He's almost dead from breathing in air pollution
He tried to vote but to him there's no solution
Chorus: Living just enough, just enough for the
     city…yeah, yeah, yeah!
I hope you hear inside my voice of sorrow
And that it motivates you to make a better tomorrow
This place is cruel nowhere could be much colder
If we don't change the world will soon be over
Chorus: Living just enough, stop giving just
     enough for the city! (Stevie wonder, 1973)

Wonder's "Living for the City" was a popular hit, but his tribute to Martin Luther King Jr., "Happy Birthday," had one of the largest impacts on African Americans. The single was written and produced by Stevie Wonder in 1981 for the Motown label. Wonder was a key figure in the campaign to have the birthday of Martin Luther King Jr. become a national holiday, and created this song-anthem to make the cause known. The song was not a Billboard hit but still remains the customary Happy Birthday song to sing to honor African American peoples' birthdays.

For Wonder to compose such a strong political message in a so-called celebratory fun song was amazing in his efforts for community building toward making M. L. King's holiday. After the song was composed and became heard, it probably had an impact on former President Ronald Reagan to approve the creation of the holiday on November 2, 1983; January 20, 1986 was the first official celebration of Martin Luther King Day. At these annual M. L. King Day events, all people of various nationalities and age groups join hand and hand and sing songs like "Lift Every Voice and Sing," "We Shall Overcome," and to the festivities' highlighted song when everyone sings "Happy Birthday" with a smile on their face and joy in their hearts.

> You know it doesn't make much sense
> There ought to be a law against
> Anyone who takes offense
> At a day in your celebration
> 'Cause we all know in our minds
> That there ought to be a time
> That we can set aside
> To show just how much we love you
> And I'm sure you will agree
> It couldn't fit more perfectly
> Than to have a world party on the day you came
>   to be
>
> Chorus:
>
> Happy birthday to you
> Happy birthday to you
> Happy birthday (Repeat)
>
> I just never understood
> How a man who died for good
> Could not have a day that would
> Be set aside for his recognition
> Because it should never be
> Just because some cannot see
> The dream as clear as he
> That they should make it become an illusion
> And we all know everything
> That he stood for time will bring
> For in peace our hearts will sing
> Thanks to Martin Luther King

[Chorus]

Why has there never been a holiday
Where peace is celebrated all throughout the world
The time is overdue
For people like me and you
You know the way to truth
Is love and unity to all God's children
It should be a great event
And the whole day should be spent
In full remembrance
Of those who lived and died for the oneness of
     all people
So let us all begin
We know that love can win
Let it out don't hold it in Sing it loud as you can.

[Chorus]

(Written by Stevie Wonder, 1981)

Chapter 6

Healing the World through Music

"Music is medicine for the soul" (Nordoff Robbins, 2012).
The healing that takes place behind playing or listening
to music is more than words can do justice.

It has been most interesting in my research to discover artists that believed in healing the world through music and finding such a person in the world of pop music. In the 1990s there was a new king of Black music, Michael Jackson—a true entertainer who not only commanded the stage but had a massive following. But some may not have known that Jackson was always a conscious participant in making the world a better place.

Michael Joseph Jackson lived from August 29, 1958 to June 25, 2009 and was a global popular culture figure for over four decades. Jackson composed hits like "Beat It," "Billie Jean," and "Thriller," but his songs of consciousness and healing helped to change pop music, too. Songs like "Man in the Mirror" (1987), "Heal the World" (1991), and "Earth Song" (1995) left his mark on music and society. It was not just about money or making a hit song but changing the world and helping people see the need to heal our planet. The song that probably had the greatest impact on the world is "We Are the World."

"We Are the World" was recorded in 1985 by an all-star cast of American musicians and singers for Africa famine relief and was produced by Quincy Jones. The songwriters were Michael Jackson and Lionel Richie and the song has sold at least ten million copies worldwide. Released as a single, the song gained worldwide commercial success and became the fastest-selling American pop single in history. The song had first been commissioned by Harry Belafonte to be written by Stevie Wonder, Lionel Richie, and Michael Jackson, but Wonder was busy at the time, so Richie and Jackson composed it. Michael, as told by LaToya, his sister, wrote the majority of the lyrics, maybe up to 99 percent (Campbell, 1994).

It all started a few days before Christmas in 1984 when Harry Belafonte was watching a television news report on the famine in Africa. Learning that twenty-nine of the thirty-six most impoverished nations in the world were in Africa and 150 million people faced a massive food shortage, Belafonte decided to do something about it. He made a call to Ken Kragen, who managed Kenny Rogers (who had been committed to the cause of world hunger), and Lionel Richie who at the time was one of the hottest hit songwriters. Belafonte was hoping to have top Black performers spearhead this music project to raise funds for Africa. After Richie and Jackson agreed to write the song, a studio was needed and a great producer. Quincy Jones decided to come on board, and Belafonte was able to lock down a date—January 28—the night of the American Music Awards when there was going to be many musical stars in town. The A&M recording studio was large enough to hold a mass choir of stars, and two hours after the end of the award show—10:00 p.m.—was the set time to begin this historic project. A few weeks before the recording date, the song still had not been written. Richie finally brought Jackson two melodic ideas on tape, Michael moved on it, and that night he went to the studio and completed song tracks with drums, piano, strings, and lyrics. Then the two—Richie and Jackson—got back together and put the lyrics in order. Jones pushed Richie and Jackson to write the song for a sea of voices, something grand and not too fast (around nineteen beats a minute), and something that would be considered an anthem.

Forty-five top American recording artists joined together on that Monday night—January 28, 1985—to record "We Are the

World," a song written by Michael Jackson and Lionel Richie to aid those who were suffering in Africa. Some of the celebrities present were Paul Smith, Diana Ross, Stevie Wonder, Smokey Robinson, Ray Charles, Tina Turner, Billy Joel, Kenny Loggins, Cyndi Lauper, James Ingram, Dionne Warwick, Al Jarreau, Huey Lewis, Anita and Ruth Pointer, and many more. It was terrific and meaningful to have such top recording artists volunteer their time and efforts to make a difference through a song (Breskin, 1985).

The Healing Power of Music

In the study of music, traditional higher education tends to focus degrees in performance, composition, and education disciplines. Colleges do offer music therapy classes but usually not taught by music instructors or in the music department. Most music majors (including myself) did not take courses on the functional uses of music and did not learn about its powers to heal. Theory and ear training, history and appreciation classes, instrumental private lessons, and recital hall were the typically assigned areas, but there were no courses for understanding what music is. My history professor would suggest the notions of music having special therapeutic powers as *hocus-pocus* myths and focused on teaching students about the European elite composers, since the rest of the world was, as my professor would say, *primitive*. There are many essential aspects of music to learn. Personally, it seems insulting not to know or learn about the powers of music as an art form or about how great it can be to perform. Again, this is another example of art for art's sake and not about how music has real meaning or purpose. Around the world there are similarities in music. There are songs of worship and ritual, work and play, love and courtship, and healing and wellness. It is only in the western societies, and mainly American scholars, who have not accepted music as a holistic method toward healing and wellness.

The average heartbeat of an adult is around seventy-two beats per minute. The body's rhythms are in a repeating cycle; the blood pressure pulse rate may increase in the morning and throughout the day as the temperature increases, the decline in the evening. Sleep also comprised of repetitive cycles of about a ninety-minute duration. The body must be tuned like an instrument in the orchestra. For instance, arthritis symptoms are usually worst in the early morning or late evening. People who work graveyard shifts seem to have more fatal diseases than those who do not. And being in touch with your breath is very important. The word *health* is associated with inhaling and wholeness; the breath is the life force, or energy, that operates your health. Learning the proper methods of inhaling and exhaling is not as simple as one might think. Taking full breaths may help in calming and strengthening your body. The heartbeat and breathing is the music of the body (Gioia, 2006).

The first healing song heard by most people is the nursery rhyme or lullaby that a mother sings to her newborn and unborn child, and maybe the earliest melody that most humans sang was *Ma* (high tone) and *ma* (low tone). This vibrating sound *mmmm* is universal when referring to mothers. In Swahili, it is *mama*; in Zulu, *umami;* in German, *mutter;* in Cambodian, *mai;* and in Arabic, it is *umm*. Biologists speculate that the similarities in various languages are due to the sound of *mmmm* which may derive from the mouth movements of an infant suckling the mother. Interestingly, an infant's inner ear develops faster than any other part of the body (Gioia, 2006).

Before humans imitated any sound on or through an object, the human body was the primal musical instrument and rhythm was already within us. Rhythms have been used to cure diseases. Musical healers have recognized that song and, more importantly, rhythm, enhances the curing process. Throughout many traditional African cultures, the magician is a musician, and the musician is a magician. But the song was more powerful than the science of magic in creating community cohesion and unity of purpose. A song is more communal, while magic is more solitary and individualistic. Music, maybe the most potent tool to involve the entire community in the health and wellness process, can create necessary alliances for the patient and the community to heal. No other force like music and song possesses the power to engage cohesion and purpose in groups, bringing individuals into the greater picture and "making them emotionally predisposed to work together" (Gioia, 2006, pp. 176).

The research on the relationship between science and song has scientists from all over the world studying the powers of music. Archaeologists have unearthed flutes made from the bones of animals by Neanderthals, now considered the world's oldest instruments. However, according to Elena Mannes, author of *The Power of Music*, "The act of human singing may have begun as long as 250,000 years ago" (Mannes, 2011, p. xvi). What seems to be universal across cultures is that how children call their mothers—ma-ah or mommy—is a simple two-syllable falling musical phrase. Maybe because the American society is very visual, people are often more aware of what they see than what they hear.

The vibration of sound can penetrate the human body. A musical sound or note has a vibration that is very regular, unlike a sound considered a noise which produces a chaotic and irregular sound wave. An aspect of *organized sound*, or music, is intervals—the relationship between tones and frequencies. When a violin string is plucked, it creates a tone containing other frequencies within it. These frequencies that are higher than the original note are called overtones. The Pythagorean mathematical discovery of the relationship of the overtones is made by dividing a string in half and plucking it to produce an octave. By separating the string so two-thirds vibrate, you get a perfect fifth of the original tone, and when three-quarters of the string vibrates, you have perfect fourth (Mannes, 2011).

Another quality of music rooted in math is rhythm. The average resting heartbeat for adults ranges from sixty to eighty beats per minute, and the normal walking step is 120 steps to the minute which is the tempo that most marches possess (such as the song "Star and Stripes Forever"). Music with a faster tempo raises the heart rate, whether the genre is pop, hip-hop, or classical. Elena Mannes, in her book *The Power of Music*, further elaborates that we, humans, *entrain* to a rhythmic beat. There is synchronization between the rhythmic cycles in which this entrainment occurs, in the same way that two clock pendulums synchronize when they are swinging at different rates and eventually swing at the same speed when placed together (Mannes, 2011).

How the emotions are affected by music is still not clear, but music shows evidence across time and cultures that it brings people together: in prayer, in war, for romance, and to soothe broken hearts. Scientists recognize that music's effect on the body, brain, and our emotions cannot be separated. Music is central to our very identity and sense of self, to our physiology and psychology. Music has an impact on our behavioral or cognitive capacity for adapting, surviving, and reproducing, on mothers calming babies, and maybe most critically, on helping to build community (Mannes, 2011).

Archaeologists, in 2008, found fragments of flutes carved from the bones of swains dating back to thirty-five thousand years ago, then shortly after that found an even older flute with four finger holes carved from an ivory tusk of a mammoth. And later, in 2009, another flute was found containing five finger holes which demonstrated that human beings of the Stone Age had a musical culture. These flutes are said to be very easy to play and display beautiful pure tones, capable of producing many notes to perform an array of various songs. According to the archaeologist Steven Mithen, Neanderthals could make a wide range of vocalizations but they were probably not speaking a language to communicate. Mithen believes Neanderthals actually sang in musical or holistic phrases to convey their feelings or emotions, and he also believes that Homo sapiens in Africa—who are our most direct ancestors—used this communication system. Steven Mithen (2005) also has pointed out that in traditional societies, music was an essential part of human existence. He explains that it is hard to understand international languages but easier to engage with foreign music through the emotions it produces. Mithen believes music was used to build group identity (Mithen, 2005).

In the area of quantum field theory, Stephon Alexander, a physicist and musician, believes there is a deep connection between music and geometry. The quantum field theory is like an orchestra where the vibration of the field gives rise to various forms of matter. Physics in this way is a lot like music where there is an overall effect of the whole. It does seem quite remarkable that music is at the core of life and that scientists are finding more and more relationships between music and the universe. NASA has conducted experiments using the electromagnetic vibrations of planets. The sounds are considered strange but pleasant, and scientists even realized that the earth has a hum, that all objects have a natural frequency at which to vibrate (Mannes, 2011). It is remarkable that science, beauty, and biology meet through music.

Many scientists now are convinced that for music to be most useful as a prescription for healing, it must become an interactive tool. The research points to proving that making music can change the brain. Music is ranked at the highest level of the fine arts because it ministers to human welfare. Music has operated as a healing force since the beginning of human history, and most healers are musicians. In many African cultures, music and healing joined together. There are studies in Zimbabwe, Malawi, Ghana, and other sub-Saharan African nations that show how intense music can alter one's state of mind. And it is in this altered consciousness that a healer exorcises a spirit or a sickness where music can guard against illness or something terrible happening.

Music is indeed an integral part of being human, and music can teach us many things about life. Music has a deeply rooted social purpose; it is not for you alone, it is meant to share with others. Music forms community; it is used daily to bring people together. Music builds personal well-being and the well-being of groups. If we do not recognize the importance of engaging people in music, we will lose an essential aspect of the human experience.

Music is crucial in the daily lives of most people in the world and has been throughout human history. Anyone who wants to understand human nature, the interaction between brain and culture, evolution and society, has to take a close look at the role that music has held in the lives of humans and at the way that music and people coevolved. I have read that Americans tend to spend more money on music than they do on prescription drugs or sex, and the average American hears more than five hours of music per day. *The World in Six Songs* by Daniel Levitin (2008) explains the evolution of music and the brain over tens of thousands of years and across the six inhabited continents. Levitin's knowledge and consideration of music's diversity states that there is a set of functions which music performs in human relations. These different functions of music have influenced the evolution of human emotion, reason, and spirit across distinct intellectual and cultural histories. The six types of songs discussed in Levitin's book that have shaped human nature are *friendship, joy, comfort, knowledge, religion, and love songs.* As I tend to agree with all of Levitin's song types, this examination will focus more on Levitin's research about religion and how songs of faith and devotion have shaped my view of life and death (Levitin, 2008).

In the common conception that humans possess abilities that make us uniquely human, language is often trotted out as a crowning achievement, with religion and music not far behind. This is contradicted by the newest research which finds that what is unique about being human is our ability to discuss and plan activities that commemorate and celebrate. Humans mourn their dead and typically with elaborate rituals; sometimes solemnly, sometimes joyfully, almost always accompanied by music. Humans imbue burying their dead with a cultural and spiritual component. A ceremony is a uniquely human invention which commemorates important events like birth, marriage, and death. These events are externalized as social memory, and when marked by music, they become even more firmly instantiated in both our personal and collective memory (Durkheim, 1976).

There is a particular kind of music—songs associated with religion, ritual, and belief—that served as a necessary function in creating early human social systems and societies. Like music, faith is in all human communities. In spite of vast differences in beliefs, practices, and geographical location, no known human culture lacks religion. It may not be possible to distinguish ritual from religion clearly, and perhaps the distinction is not as important as understanding how they relate to one another, how rituals became bound up into religion (Dawkins, 1965). Rituals involve repetitive movement. Human rituals are a cognitive component of self-consciousness which serves as a form of communication. Anthropologist Roy

Rappaport defined ritual as "acts of display through which one or more participants transmit information concerning their physiological, psychological, or sociological states, either to themselves or one or more of their participants." The story of ritual is intimately bound up with music, which almost always accompanies it, and with human nature (Levitin, 2008).

Several scientific studies have shown that there exist neural regions that might be called *God centers*. When they are electrically stimulated when we pray for the health of a dying loved one, the termination of the prayer confers a great psychological advantage: it allows us to stop worrying. We breathe a sigh of release and affirm that "It's in God's hands, fate is decided." Religion grew out of this desire to make sense of the world. Religions trained us and taught us to accept society-building, interpersonally bonding propositions. Ceremonies with music reaffirm the propositions, and the music sticks within our heads, reminding us of what we believe and what we have agreed. Rappaport (1971) defined religion as "sets of sacred beliefs held in common by groups of people and…the more or less standard actions (rituals) that are undertaken concerning these beliefs." He defines *sacred* as those beliefs that are unverifiable through ordinary physical means or the key five senses—the belief or faith in things that are not corporeal but that can influence the course of our lives (Rappaport, 1971).

At this time in my life, I tend to go to more funerals than weddings. There are known favorite songs that I have grown up hearing and playing. Some of the most popular are: "Precious Lord," "Fly Away," "His Eye Is On A Sparrow," and "Going Up Yonder," but still one of the most beloved is "Amazing Grace." Recently, I attended one of my childhood friends' father's funeral and found myself wrapped up in the music, maybe because the musician who played has been a friend of my family for as long as I can remember. Frank Fisher has played in some of the greatest jazz big bands, including Duke Ellington and Count Basie. At this time, Frank is ninety years old and he decided to play his muted trumpet without any accompaniment. (I have played several funerals in the past on the piano with Mr. Fisher.) He played for his musical selection a solo rendition of

"Nobody Knows the Trouble I've Seen" which sounded so sweet it brought tears to my eyes. The beauty of the trumpet tone and the slow rhythmic pace of the melody sang out more explicitly than any words a singer could have expressed at that moment. It reminded me how music leaves a lasting impression, and no matter the song style, the when, why, and how the music played is most significant toward its effect. For the recession song, the pianist played "Amazing Grace," and Mr. Fisher chimed in on trumpet. What a moving and emotional end to a lovely ceremony to honor the departed family and friends. All that was left to say was "Amen!"

Music is so memorable. It is incredible how people can still sing along with a song on the radio which they have not heard in thirty to forty years; songs can serve as mnemonic devices for knowledge of civilizations, rituals, and religious practices. One reason can be because of the multiple embedded cues of melody and rhythm constrained by form and style as encoded in a series of statistical maps and, ultimately, statistical inferences.

A *song,* by definition, is a musical composition intended or adapted for singing, a broad category that includes anything we might sing. African drum music has a vital role in the daily lives of millions of people, though some may not understand how these rhythmic forms of expression are songs since it does not always involve singing. However, most popular styles of music—rock, pop, jazz, and hip-hop—would not exist without the African drumming from which they evolved. The word *song* is also used as a more inclusive term to stand for music in all its forms—any music that people make, with or without melody, with or without lyrics. Whether we are singing in church choirs, playing instruments in school orchestras, or participating in a drum circle, we are participating in forms of community building and healing through song.

Drum Circles

Drum circles are a prevalent form of music therapy and community engagement designed to allow every participant to have an equal place with no sense of ranking from good to bad. Drum circle therapy traces back to ancient techniques of historical African civilizations. For instance, the Yoruba people of Nigeria in West Africa practice an intricate system of medicine in which the community calls upon the cosmic energy or divinity of a deity or an orisha. In this ceremony, sacred drums and rhythms are played to summon the ancestral orisha associated with the beat. These rhythms are thought of as prayers offered as a way to praise and evoke the spirit's presence. From these ceremonies, participants have an increase in life force energy, generate more balance and alignment, find inner peace, and enhance satisfaction with life (Nunez, 2016).

The circle also has its origin in Africa and is even linked to hip-hop. The ring helped preserve the elements that have characterized the foundation of African American music: calls, cries, and hollers; call and response devices; blue notes; offbeat melodic phrasing; hand clapping, foot patting; game rivalry; and apart playing. As far as hip-hop is concerned, artists before their performance still form a circle to pray and honor the Higher Spirit. Most hip-hop performance rituals are also based on the enclosing of the performers by the audience; for example, break dancing and MC battles are still presented this way. Even while dancers and rappers perform, they speak of being possessed or having out-of-body experiences. The circle is found in dancing, drumming, and singing which makes it indispensable as a conceptual frame in which all African American music can be explored.

There are various systems of drumming: freestyle, recreational, ceremonial, and therapeutic. All of these categories may be restorative and promote health. These drumming styles each have specific elements that make them suitable for particular purposes. However, the one that may best maintain healing and wellness is ceremonial/medicinal.

Freestyle and recreational drum circles are gatherings done for fun and leisure. Usually, these drum circles are held in public areas, with no facilitator leading so anyone can participate. Recreational drum circles may have a facilitator guiding the collective in activities and drum patterns. In both drumming practices, participants usually experience a sense of wellness.

Ceremonial/medicinal drumming is based closer to cultural and spiritual belief systems which engenders the community through sacred space. The participants playing drums around the circle are engaged in the process to expand awareness, elevate consciousness, commune with ancestral spirits, and restore physical and mental balance. Although many of the intended purposes of drumming have been forgotten or lost over the course of time, a good starting point for a drum circle is to have a facilitator who has some training and practice in drumming groups and to establish an organized and substantial space of support and caring for the participants.

In my experience, facilitated drum circles are a great way of bringing students and mainly Black males together to promote a safe, stress-free, and entertaining environment and give them a sense of empowerment. Facilitating a group of students playing drums increases concentration and focus which helps to develop communication skills and encourages them to listen and communicate effectively with each other.

The primary reason why I try to create drum circles, whether it is in the community or on the college campus, has little to do with the ability or musical experience of the participants, but instead relies mainly on the quality of the emerging relationships through making music together that develops naturally. The expertise of drumming in a circle with others, especially playing with bare hands, is very therapeutic. This activity helps people express and address issues that otherwise are difficult to share. It allows each participant to create an external and physical outlet of whatever frustration that he may be dealing with at that time.

Music therapy has become an essential avenue in working with African American mental health issues. Theorists of music therapy (Ruud, 1998; Stige, 2020) have argued that music and culture are inseparable, and that hip-hop and rap music has a vital role in today's social transformation of young men of color (Lightstone, 2012). Mental health issues for African American and Latino youth usually occur from experiences with growing up in poverty; dropping out of high school; having a criminal record; absentee fathers; teenage mothers; high exposure to violence, drugs, and alcohol; involvement with gangs; have witnessed death; and suffering from post-traumatic stress disorder (Brooks et al., 2010).

Traditionally, there has been a stigma toward mental illness in African American and Latino communities. As young males, we often grow up with a sense of toughness. To conceal hurt, hide emotions, and deal with your problems. No crying, whining, or telling on others, especially your siblings or your friends. Mostly, the only feeling we show and were acknowledged by our peers as okay was anger. Therefore, to seek mental therapy was shameful and looked down upon. Also, most mental health professionals are White and not trusted in the communities of color (Alvarez, 2012). Due to the lack of options for the youth of color, particularly Black and Latino males, alternative models are needed. Rap or hip-hop therapy is currently found to be highly useful in improving mental health outcomes, especially with urban youth of color (Allen, 2005; DeCarlo and Hockman; Tyson, 2003). In the next chapter, I will offer a brief outline and summary of hip-hop music and culture and its role in social justice and community healing.

Chapter 7

Social and Cultural Justice through Hip-Hop

The arts and humanities are not just there to be consumed when you have a free moment. We need them like medicine. They help us live.
—*President Barack Obama*

*H*ip-hop music has historical and traditional ties to African culture. From the great oral and vocal master storytellers of the jeli or griot to the musical concepts of call and response and the powerful poetic rhythms of the talking drum, all these African traditions have led to rap/hip-hop music. Most of the American musical genres primarily influenced by African culture, such as gospel, blues, jazz, soul, funk, and hip-hop, have all been connected to the social and cultural justice of the Black community.

Hip-hop is more than just a music genre. It has become a robust global economy and a movement. It follows the line of African traditions in its performance techniques and becomes the voice of the people. It is the third significant Black movement in the USA which focused on art as the medium of expression to share and release the social and cultural injustices plagued on people of African descent for the last century, along with the Harlem Renaissance and the Black Arts movements.

The Harlem Renaissance movement, also known as the New Negro movement, took place mainly in New York's Harlem district from roughly 1918 to 1937, and was considered the first significant

Black movement in America that placed art at the core of its existence. It gave rise to jazz music, visual art, and all Black theater and dance performances, but was led by the literary masters—the poets and novelists. Alain Locke, one of the architects of the movement and a leading Rhodes Scholar, termed this time as a New Awakening or New Negro movement. Locke wanted to give force and credit to the brilliance of creative artists and writers to prove to the world the greatness of the African American. Even though there were many outstanding musicians, like Duke Ellington and Fats Waller or incredible painters like Aaron Douglas and Jacob Lawrence, this movement was led, like most African American art movements, by the literary artists—poets like Claude McKay (*If We Must Die*) and the legendary Langston Hughes (*I've Known Rivers*)—maybe because African people are moved by the power of the word, from the sermon to the comedian, and the politician to the MC (master of ceremonies presenter).

An art movement means people working together to advance their shared social, cultural, and political views through an artistic or creative idea. Again, in America, there have been three arts movements that were led by African descendants: the Harlem Renaissance, the Black Arts, and the Hip-hop movement. The Black Arts Movement was from 1965 to 1977; also was centered in Harlem, New York. The key principal of the Black Arts Movement was Amiri Baraka (LeRoi Jones) who authored the text *Blues People*. Baraka was thought of as the father of the Black Arts Movement after he opened the Black Arts Repertory Theatre in Harlem in 1965. The Black Arts Movement was an offshoot of the Black Power movement associated with Malcolm X (or El Haij Malik El Shabazz). After Malcolm's assassination in 1965, the Black Power movement split into various camps. Two of the best known were the Revolutionary Nationalists, represented by the Black Panther Party of the Oakland Bay Area, and the Cultural Nationalists, which was a group of artists, musicians, and writers. These Black artists created a public and cultural space for Black art to be by and about Black people as a means to awaken the consciousness of Black people to liberation practices and agenda. The impact of the movement was expressed best through the poetry and theater.

As in Africa, poetry was used like drums as a transportation device. To counter that thought, Nketia (1974) states that rhythm is the primary focus of drumming, but the aesthetic appeal of drumming lies in the rhythmic and melodic elements. Wilson (1992) further implies that the drum patterns of the preexisting repertoire of the master drummers in many African cultures is based on musical models derived from selected genres of oral poetry.

The power of telling stories, prose, or poetry with the accompaniment of music has long cultural roots for African Americans and is one of the antecedents of hip-hop music. In West Africa, a common form of documentation of history is done orally. Not because Africans did not have the ability or skill to write it down in books, but because of the industrial slave trade that ripped Africans and their belongings from their families and land that made it more important for people to know their history through song and story. These custodians of their societies' historical and cultural knowledge are called jeli (an indigenous Mande term) or the more popular term griot (a French term of origin).

Performance styles and practices of jeli or griots come in various forms, such as historical or fictional narrative, praising/honoring, and advising and ridicule. Usually, the performance is outdoors in a shared public space, open for the community to join. These performers' preferred instrument is the kora, but some may also play hand drums or djembe. Another ancient African singing tradition, known as gawella which is a gossip poem sung by Yoruba woman, is done when two women are arguing and want to vent in public. The galla sang in a public space marketplace where other women of the community could hear. A key performance concept used in modern American music that also has African origins is call and response. Like: "If I say hey, you say ho! Hey, ho." This West African music concept of engaging the audience together with the performer is a practice among African people. It applies to the philosophy that unites the two sides as one.

Credited as the father of rap music, Clive Campbell (DJ Kool Herc), whose family was from Jamaica, used a rapping manner of spoken injections over rhythmic breaks in songs, a style known to

Jamaicans as toasting. A toast is a form of verbal art made popular by Jamaican youth that tends to celebrate the outlaw. The outlaw could refer to act of violence or to a *baadman* who is becoming successful in an unjust society and how to overcome the racist and discriminatory obstacles. Kool Herc states that "Hip-hop is the voice of this generation" (Chang, 2005) and how it has become a dominant force to make a collective stand and statement.

The four elements of hip-hop that are most discussed are DJing, B-boying, graffiti, and MCing, but the fifth and maybe most important is knowledge! DJing (disc jockey) is supplying the rhythm or beat aspects. The term relates to early radio personalities of rhythm and blues and rock and roll of the 1940s and fifties who provided the discs, set the vinyl records on the turntable, and introduced the song to the listening audience. Their style was fresh and provocative, and most listeners were confused about whether the disc jockey was White or Black. A DJ was the most critical element in old school rap. He brought the music, which consisted of crates of albums, a PA system with massive size speakers, two turntables to keep the music constant, and a microphone to keep the crowd *lit*, hyped, or engaged. In my travels to Africa, the gatekeeper of every village is usually a traditional drummer. He welcomes you through ancient rhythms that speak or correlate with the traditional languages of his village. He is usually an elder that knows the customs and traditions, and the proper response when you hear the drummer calling is to dance!

B-boying is the dance element B that represents break-dancers or *break boys* that would accompany or show up to all the DJ's parties and dance on the instrumental or percussion breaks of the song. Where there is music, there is dance! In most public settings in Africa, music forms a physical response, as in a dance—moving your body in either coordinated or uncoordinated actions through the feeling of the music. A common aspect of traditional African dance is centered and honors the earth. So many of the dance styles focused on the core: pelvic and butt areas. Knees are bent and there are many gestures to the ground. Some forms lie on the ground and spin around. The most important beats and tones are the lowest because the sound vibrates the room and puts emphasis on the *core*. Africans also employed a form of tactical combat dancing called capoeira. Capoeira has been compared to break dancing and b-boying because of its similarities in style, movement, and purpose.

In many enslaved societies in America, the drum was outlawed. It was replaced with doing beats with hands, feet, and body, such as hambone, a popular form of expression: children clapping and rhyming in song. An example is Miss Mary Mack. Tap dancing was also a key form doing the 1920s to 1950s, as it showcases Black tappers who were able to speak with their feet, supply the rhythms, or even replace the drummer with the feet beats. Most of these tap dancers were good trap drummers as well. Another note of interest is the connection of basketball to hip-hop. The basketball bouncing off a gymnasium floor has a great acoustic low bass sound. In basketball, the ball handler uses the bounce of the ball in a syncopated rhythm to throw off his defender. Some say this is a dance of diversion between the offensive player with the ball and the defender trying to stop the opponent from scoring (or embarrassing him in front of others). Break dancing also shows a strong relationship to capoeira. Eventually, b-boying was replaced with the video diva which is usually a beautiful young lady with a *banging body* in a seductive dress (usually a bikini) to accentuate all her body assets. However, still one of the essential elements of hip-hop music is how you dance or move to it. The beginnings of hip-hop were to get and keep the party going which means getting everybody to have a good time on the dance floor. There was no fighting, gangbanging, drug and alcohol use, or violence allowed in these early party scenes led by the original of rap DJs—Kool Herc, Afrika Bambaataa, and Grandmaster Flash.

Graffiti also has African origins, but out of all the elements in hip-hop, it is the one that may not have always had a direct connection to rap or hip-hop music, as graffiti was also a part of the rock, punk, and heavy metal scene. Although visual art and artists had played a significant role in the Harlem Renaissance and the Black Arts Movement, most of the critical graffiti artists were non-Black males. However, there is evidence of graffiti during ancient Egyptian civilizations. The term is derived from a Greek word *graphein* which translates in English as "scratching." Egyptians were known to honor their ancestors through these wall engravings or scratchings as forms of respect and remembrance. The term *graffiti* refers to short, anonymous, unauthorized drawing or writing on a blank surface that can be seen by the public or in public spaces.

MCing, master of ceremonies, was once an added flair to the hip-hop party scene, but it was the DJ who was the essential element. However, the MC was soon crowned as the king of the hip-hop world. The MC does share direct characteristics of the jeli and griot from West Africa, but they follow other storytelling genres, such as the folklore traditions of the trickster who was considered a clever person or animal able to manipulate others to get what he wants. This character has a long tradition in the Black storytelling community. Whether the link to the MC is chronicling history, toasting, or honoring others, boasting as in praising self or signifying. The setting is most often in a public space (or cipher). A cipher, also spelled as cypher, is the shared space in hip-hop in which people create and engage with each other. A cipher is a literal and most likely a circular area that participants create when they are dancing, rapping, or performing other engaging exchanges through hip-hop.

Understanding hip-hop culture is a critical discourse of engaging and teaching in higher education. Many of today's college students, especially Black and Latinos, are active participants who listen to rap music and are invested in its genealogies, study its relevancies, deconstruct its themes, and hold it as an acceptable source of knowledge parallel to college course curriculum (Petchauer, 2012).

Knowledge, culture, and overstanding (human beings' natural state of mind undisturbed by the ego), which is the fifth element of hip-hop. Afrika Bambaataa, one of hip-hop's innovators, explains that the fifth element really is the core of what hip-hop is all about—to unite and learn about your culture. Here is an excerpt from Bambaataa, written in 1995:

> Yes, there are many wrongs in the worldwide hip-
> hop community, but there are also many aspects
> of positivity within the hip-hop community that
> the media or trade magazines rarely focus upon.

Many of you in hip-hop culture don`t even listen to the rappers who are trying hard to wake your asses up to what is going on in the bigger scale than of what you see in your neighborhoods, their message goes in one ear and out the other.

The media does play a big role in destroying the hip-hop culture movement, but many of you in the hip-hop community are the biggest enemies of hip-hop and you will be the ones who will help the enemies of hip-hop to destroy it, or to bring it back underground, because of your ignorance of knowledge of hip-hop. This has started the difference between *old school* and *new school.*

To myself (Afrika Bambaataa) there is only one school and that`s the learning, evolving, going through the different phases or cycles school of hip-hop. That is the real hip-hop school. A lot of you in the world of hip-hop better start looking at the problems in your own backyard as well as the world, because while you are enjoying yourselves etc. there are many plots being sprung to destroy hip-hop in the world. Because many people in government look at hip-hop music and its culture as a radical music that gets straight to the point and music that will wake up the youth and young adults throughout the world. They can also use hip-hop to backfire and destroy it. You can believe what I`m saying. But time will tell and I see what you see not." (Bambaataa, *Bomb Hip-Hop* magazine #38, March 1995)

Hip-hop music, too, is one of the most effective modern tools used to fight and mobilize Black youth around the world on social injustices and equality concerns. One of the reasons hip-hop is such a valid art form to use as a social justice empowerment strategy, or as a way to get youth involved in their civic and moral responsibilities, is because all one needs is a melodic idea and rhythm, a voice, and a beat. One does not need a musical instrument or even a turntable. When it comes down to it, all that is needed is lyrical flow.

The hip-hop generation, according to Bakari Kitwana from his award-winning book of the same name, includes young people that were born between 1965 and 1984. Black youth of this hip-hop generation's identity has been shaped by at least six major sociopolitical forces: (1) the visibility of Black youth within the molding and shaping of popular culture; (2) the emergence of globalization, in the 1980s and 1990s, has significantly influenced the worldview of hip-hop generations; (3) the contradictory persistence of segregation in an America that preaches democracy and inclusion; (4) the impact of public policy regarding criminal justice, especially in regards to policy that has clear racial implications; (5) the media representation of young Blacks as being negative and violent; and (6) the final force that is shaping the hip-hop generation is the overall shift in the quality of life for young Blacks during the 1980s and 1990s (Kitwana, 2002).

Hip-Hop Movement

It seems the commonality in each of the significant arts movements by African Americans—Harlem Renaissance, Black Arts, and hip-hop movements—is use of the three categories of art: visual, performing, and literary. However, the writers and poets have led all three movements. The poet, speaker, commendatory, preacher, comedian, actor, professor, and singer have always held high status in the Black community. This is probably due to the platform these personalities have to express their thoughts and feelings toward social justice and equality. There are many similarities between these Black art movements, however there are some significant differences as well. Maybe they are best expressed by this analogy: the Negro movement (Harlem Renaissance). We, as people of color, knocked on the door, asking "Can we come?" although we still went naturally to the back door. The next movement, we demanded a seat at the table, with our Afros and political agendas. Finally, now we come tearing down the door, burning the place up, and replacing it with something new. I interpret that the Harlem Renaissance was an attempt to impress White people with Black artistic and scholarly abilities to show that they were just as good as a form of assimilation (especially since more light complexions were acceptable over darker hues). During the Black Arts period, we understood more of our art direction and identity but still had no true economic equality. The hip-hop movement is finally providing an economic mobility, a cultural identity, and a social platform to voice our critique and assessment of our reality. Unfortunately, everything has a price, especially when you make a deal with the devil.

A potent example of how rap and hip-hop music connect to the social justice movement is the song "Self-Destruction," a collaboration project that reflects community building and healing. The song was a part of the Stop the Violence Movement founded by KRS-One in 1989 as a response to the violence occurring in the African American communities and within hip-hop. KRS-One was affected by the killing of Scott La Rock, a founding member of KRS-One's Boogie Down Productions, and by a fan that was killed in a fight at a 1988 concert by Boogie Down Productions and Public Enemy. By the Stop the Violence Movement, he would advance a vision of hip-hop that could restore what the original principles of hip-hop were. KRS-One and D-Nice of Boogie Down Productions produced the song, and Hank Shocklee of the Bomb Squad was credited as an associate producer. This song marked one of the first true collaborations by many of the current leaders of rap music and featured the following: KRS-One, D-Nice, Ms. Melodie, Stesasonic, Kool Moe Dee, MC Lyte, Doug E. Fresh (who also created the chorus of the song), Just Ice, Heavy D, and Public Enemy—Chuck D and Flavor Flav. The song debuted at number one on Billboard's Hot Rap Songs for five consecutive weeks. However, in the same year, Public Enemy released "Fight the Power" which is considered by many as the greatest hip-hop social justice rap song.

[KRS-One]
Well, today's topic, self-destruction
It really ain't the rap audience that's buggin
It's one or two suckas, ignorant brothers
Trying to rob and steal from one another
You get caught in the mid
So to crush the stereotype here's what we did
We got ourselves together
So that you could unite and fight for what's right
Not negative 'cause the way we live is positive
We don't kill our relatives."

[MC Delight (Stetsasonic)]
Pop pop pop
When it's shot who's to blame?
Headlines, front page, and rap's the name
MC Delight here to state the bottom line
That black-on-black crime was way before our
    time."

[Kool Moe Dee]
Took a brother's life with a knife as his wife
Cried 'cause he died a trifling death
When he left his very last breath
Was I slept so watch your step
Back in the sixties our brothers and sisters were
    hanged
How could you gang-bang?
I never ever ran from the Ku Klux Klan
And I shouldn't have to run from a black man
Cause that's

Chorus

[D-Nice]
It's time to stand together in a unity

Cause if not then we're soon to be
Self-destroyed, unemployed
The rap race will be lost without a trace
Or a clue but what to do
Is stop the violence and kick the science
Down the road that we call eternity
Where knowledge is formed and you'll learn to be
Self-sufficient, independent
To teach to each is what rap intended
But society wants to invade
So do not walk this path they laid.

Chorus

[Ms. Melodie]
I'm Ms. Melodie and I'm a born again rebel
The violence in rap must cease and seckle
If we want to develop and grow to another level
We can't be guinea pigs for the devil
The enemy knows, they're no fools
Because everyone knows that hip-hop rules
So we gotta get a grip and grab what's wrong
The opposition is weak and rap is strong

[Doug E. Fresh]
This is all about, no doubt, to stop violence
But first let's have a moment of silence
Fresh beatboxes... Swing
Things been stated re-educated, evaluated
Thoughts of the past have faded
The only thing left is the memories of our belated
And I hate it, when
Someone dies and gets all hurt up
For a silly gold chain by a chump.
(Produced by KRS-One, D-Nice, and Hank
    Shocklee, 1988)

Kendrick Lamar

The Pulitzer Prize awarded to Kendrick Lamar on April 16, 2018, for his *DAMN* recording masterpiece was the first nonclassical, non-jazz album in the Board's seventy-five-year history to win the award. Many from the classical and jazz world questioned: why award the Pulitzer to popular music, and particularly a hip-hop artist? The decision to select the winner was made from the Pulitzer Board's jury comprised of distinguished composers, musicians, scholars of music, and music critics (Lynch, 2018).

Musical excellence should not be confined to any genre, and when injustice permeates society, an accurate way of conveying the emotions of the people is through song. Kendrick Lamar is from the tradition of artists like Marvin Gaye, Sam Cooke, Bob Marley, and Stevie Wonder who used politically charged responses to the racism, police brutality, and violence that plagues society.

As a new civil rights movement, #BlackLivesMatter has incited palpable discontent across the country due to the high-profile deaths of Trayvon Martin, Michael Brown, Tamir Rice, Eric Garner, Freddie Gray, and Walter Scott. Lamar's major hit "Alright" on his last album *To Pimp a Butterfly* has become the anthem of Black Lives Matter because of how the song critiques police brutality but still radiates positivity (Haltiwanger, 2015).

Kendrick Lamar is an outgrowth of Compton and the gangsta rap scene. He combines these elements to create music that traces the history of conscious rappers and West Coast gangsta rap. Lamar raises social awareness within his community and gives those on the outside a better understanding of the forces that created the environment in which he grew up.

In Lamar's most recent project *DAMN* released in April 2017, he struggles to balance his urge to stay true to his goals of being a positive influence with his self-acknowledged violent and boastful tendencies. In the final track of the *DAMN* album, "Duckworth," Lamar provides introspection into himself and the character of his music. He tells the story of how a man (the titular Duckworth) was robbed working at a fast food restaurant that a year before had been held up and befriended the people who had robbed it. The same people held up the store again and everyone was killed, except Duckworth. Duckworth is then revealed as Lamar's father, and Top Dawg, the founder of Lamar's label, was the robber and killer. In this track, the thought is posed that random chance brought these two people together, and if they have taken a different path, he would be left with no father and no director of his label (Rocha, 2017).

The purposes of Lamar's music are self-change and hope. He acknowledges that a vast part of his success is due in part to the gang violence and activity that he advocates against in his music. This acknowledgment acts as a claim to Lamar's social messages, with his struggle to fight his flaws, so that he can make a positive change to the world as a model for systematic change within the United States for people of color. This claim is that we all have a duty and power to enact change within ourselves, and music has to move us to change the cultural dynamics around us (Lamar, 2017).

Conclusion

Using Music Education Strategies to Foster Academic Success for African American Males in California Community Colleges

"Music education develops the creative capacities for lifelong success: Engagement, persistence, and creativity are components of higher-level thinking and complex problem solving" (Costa and Kallick, 2000).

*I*n my thirty years as a college professor of African American studies and music, I have noticed many aspects of studying the arts and particularly music that are key strategies found for successful learning. Studying art is based on creativity, aesthetic communication, and symbolism. These are the main areas I focus on in my teaching. I work on being creative in my delivery of information to students to ensure that I reach them: presenting an aesthetic view of life in how I communicate the lecture, as well as using symbolism, metaphors, and analogies in my teaching for students to develop better critical thinking skills.

The arts are viewed through three main scopes: visual, performing, and literary. In visual arts, such as painting, sculpture, and photography, one learns to develop a keen sense of lines, shapes, and dimensions of space and design. In doing these arts one can connect the art and science. For instance, geometric shapes are studied through drawings and paintings. In learning how to paint, we learn geometry and can see the world around us in ways that we might not otherwise have been able to. In the performing arts, such as music, dance, and theater, we learn sound, movement, and performance. We are able to offer a precision beyond the power of words and beyond the world of concrete visual things. Learning how to listen to what we hear and project our voices to be heard are developed in performing arts. Participating and learning literary arts helps us understand the power of words as a description to provoke thoughts, feelings, and stories to follow and frame aspects of our own lives. Education through the arts is critical in educating the whole person.

Music is multifaceted and can be useful in fulfilling many vital human needs. The practice of music education should reflect the nature of music and the quality of human interactions with it. Moreover, the aesthetic function is a vital one, but just one of several. Music encompasses our soul as a mirror that reflects how we perceive the world around us. When teaching basic music concepts, the essential elements shown are *melody, rhythm,* and *harmony.* The term *melody* is viewed as the thread that flows through the teaching lesson. The *rhythm* is the movement—the *call and response*—for students to react and participate. *Harmony* connection is when students are engaged and working together in groups or sharing information with others. My biggest joy is to see students in conversation, presenting their views about today's lesson.

To focus primarily on how to help increase African American males' success in community colleges, I am suggesting that we look closer at the cultural characteristics of African American acculturated learners. "African American students are more successful in learning environments characterized by harmony, cooperation, affect, socialization, and community" (Perry, Steele, and Hilliard, 2004). Black male students tend to benefit from a dialogical learning environment and educators who forge supportive, caring relationships with students beyond the classroom context (Delpit, 1996). Professor Silvester Henderson (Los Medanos College) is a great example of an educator who cares to teach his students right from wrong and continues to connect with his students after they have moved on. (Professor Henderson teaches vocal music at a small community college in Northern California. One of his largest ensembles is his gospel choir in which he has over a dozen Black males.) Henderson has stated that he uses gospel music as a teaching tool to show students how music can nurture and open the heart up to common humanity, as well as to encourage his students through a level of comfort and exploring new opportunities for personal growth which can lead to change (Henderson, 2017). "Many African American students are socialized to thrive in communicative environments where there is an active and improvisational interchange between speaker and audience, instead of one in which there exists a prescribed (or implied) rigid structure of communication" (Bennett, 2006). "These modes as interactive and participatory, or what often referred to as call and response" (Peterson, 2004).

Call and response is just one of the many critical strategies found in music education that can be used to foster academic achievement in African American males. Others are: a melodic style of teaching students that encompasses, dynamics, rhythmic format, to employ syncopation, timing, and the beat; and harmony, keeping students moving together but with different views of how to get there. I like to employ the *call and response* concept in my teaching. From my experience and research, there is a common pattern that African American males tend to respond to things regarding the whole picture instead of its parts. Greeting students as you enter the class also helps in appealing to the emotional tone and mood of the classroom environment. Using quotes or proverbs to begin the class session helps to motivate and entice the students to respond. This concept, referred to as *call and response*, has its origin in West African music as a means to engage the community as one. The key instrument is the *talking drum* because many African dialects have a strong emphasis on the tonal aspect of the word, and the *talking drum* has the ability by squeezing the strings (cow or goat hide) that are attached to the wooden cylinder shaped instrument that you play under your armpit to imitate these languages. For the drum to be a communal instrument requires keen listening abilities to hear the tone and rhythms and to understand the message. Being responsive to students, allowing them to ask questions or offer their perspectives helps to build a communal atmosphere. Engaging the audience through call and response is not as useful if there is no *dynamics* which is also another essential feature by accentuating areas for discussion. Not lecturing in the same tone and volume helps to develop the interest in the *melody* or theme of the lesson necessary to keep a thematic thread that flows throughout the class session.

The primary objective for excellent teaching and successful learning is for students to be cared for and engaged in the educational process. When you can be more of a performer and teach students to be more active learners through spirit, rhythm, and story, or employ musical strategies of call and response, syncopation, and harmony, then the learning process is in motion. For genuinely active learning, it is essential when both sides are learning and teaching. Do not try to control the learning environment but be the conductor—guide your students to be best learners, and they will push you to be the best teacher! I teach so that I can learn, and I learn so that I can teach!

I hope after reading this book you will continue to examine how music and songs have had an impact on your life and how music is more than just entertainment or emotional solace, it is our life connector and guide to who we are as people. It has the power to heal and transform us, both as individuals and as a collective of people, animals, and life energies.

Appendix 1

Survey on Community Building
through Song

Question Ideas:

1. What song has had the strongest impact on your life and why? (Please name the song title and artist who performs it/composed it.)

2. How much/what percentage of time is music a part of your life?

   A. 2–3 hours
   B. 4–5 hours
   C. 6–7 hours
   D. 8 hours or more

3. What role does music play in your life?

   A. Church
   B. Social
   C. Art and culture
   D. Personal enrichment
   E. Healing

4. What song do you think has had the greatest impact on humanity?

5. Ethnicity?

    A. African/African American/Black
    B. Asian
    C. White
    D. Latino
    E. Other

6. Age range?

    A. 17–18 years
    B. 19–21 years
    C. 22–25 years
    D. 26–up

7. Gender?

    A. Female
    B. Male
    C. Other

8. Education completion?

    A. High school diploma
    B. Community College
    C. AA
        1) AS
        2) University
            a) Bachelor's
            b) Master's
            c) Doctorate/professional—(attorney, clergy)

9. What style of music is your preference? (Okay to check more than once.)

    A. Classical
    B. Spiritual/gospel
    C. Blues
    D. Country
    E. Folk
    F. Funk
    G. Jazz
    H. Rock
    I. Soul
    J. R and B
    K. Hip-Hop

10. Where do you most often attend live music events?

    A. Locally—Richmond
    B. Berkeley
    C. Oakland
    D. SF
    E. Napa
    F. Other

Appendix 2

Ten Songs that had a Significant Impact on Community Building and Healing

1. "Nkosi Sikelel" (apartheid), 1897
2. "Lift Every Voice and Sing" (Harlem Renaissance era), 1900
3. "Memphis Blues" (first recording of the blues), 1912
4. "Strange Fruit" (stop lynching of African American men), 1939
5. "We Shall Overcome" (civil rights movement), 1948
6. "A Change is Gonna Come" (the end of the violence), 1964
7. "Say it Loud, I'm Black and Proud" (Black Power movement), 1968
8. "The Revolution Will Not Be Televised" (educating the community media), 1971
9. "Happy Birthday" (tribute to Martin and changed tradition), 1981
10. "We Are the World" (USA for Africa; feed the hungry), 1985

Appendix 3

Journey to the Motherland

*T*he village we visited, Tetteh-gu, was a real test in humility for all us Westerners. They had no running water or electricity, but they had order and a close-knit community. The village ambassadors took us on a brief tour and set up benches for us inside the elders' compound. They welcomed us with a short ceremony. Our tour guide, Kwesi (James), interpreted for us, as the elders poured libations and prayed for our health, wealth, and safe travel. We thanked them for sharing their community with us and left gifts, including crayons, coloring books, writing tablets, pencils, nail polish, jump ropes, and other small trinkets for the children. We also left a sizable donation for the community: about $100 or 85,000 cedis, Ghanaian currency. The elders said our donation would be used for the children's school. We took pictures and exchanged warm embraces. One of the BSAP students said he felt like he was *returning home to his village.* Unfortunately, I walked a little ahead with a small group and missed the flurry of spirited drumming and dance by the Tetteh-gu and BSAP, truly a once in a lifetime encounter.

We then set off to the Cape Coast. Luckily, it was about a three-hour bus ride away. We all had a good nap. Later that evening, after we settled into what has to be one of the best resorts in the world, the Coconut Beach Resort in Elmina, Ghana, we performed at the festival's opening ceremony. We were all in a state of awe as we listened to choir after choir perform perfect renditions of mostly hymns and other religious songs. The Ghanaians pride themselves on their choral expertise, and for good reason. They are simply spectacular. Their colorful costumes and spirited singing were uplifting. I think we were all *shaking in our boots*. We did not have the large choral presence of the other choirs. Our songs were mostly secular and we had live music and dance to accompany the singing. In spite of the technical problems with microphones and other equipment, we managed to give a good performance and engage the crowd. They especially liked "Get Down To the Music." It is pretty hard not to like that song. If you have the least bit of soul, you will want to clap your hands and tap your feet.

> To the sound of the bass slap
> Funk that'll make your toes tap
> Beat that'll make your hands clap
> Come on let's get on down, get on down, get on
>   down

We finally made it back to the resort, ate dinner, and settled into our cottage for a much needed rest. The only problem was that none of us could sleep. We were all too excited. It was almost overwhelming to touch our feet on this sacred land of our ancestors—to feel the sand between our toes, to *wade in the water of our forefathers*. We were really at home. I felt a peace I have never quite experienced before. It was magical. The majesty and beauty of the ocean simply took my breath away. Needless to say, we did not get much rest. We stayed up, sharing our personal journeys—stories of gratitude and hope—feeling the magic of it all.

Amanda Elliott

Lead vocalist, Executive Director, Richmond Main Street Initiative

African American Improvisational Music

Significant Songs from the 1900s–2010s

Styles	*Periods Performers*
Ragtime	1900s Scott Joplin, "Maple Leaf Rag"
New Blues	1910s W.C. Handy, "Memphis Blues," 1912
	1920s Mamie Smith, "Crazy Blues," 1920
Jazz	Fats Waller, "Ain't Misbehavin," 1929
	Louis Armstrong,
	"When the Saints Go Marching In," 1938
Swing	1930s Duke Ellington/Billy Strayhorn—
	"Take the A Train," 1939
	Billie Holiday, "Strange Fruit," 1939
Bebop	1940s Thelonious Monk,
	"Round Midnight," 1944
	Charlie Parker, "Now's the Time," 1945
Cool	1950s Nat "King" Cole, "Unforgettable," 1951
	Miles Davis, "All Blues," 1959
Soul	1960s Betty Carter—
	"Ain't Nothing but Soul," 1960

Avant Garde/Radical	Nina Simone, "Mississippi Goddam," 1964
Funk Fusion	1970s Herbie Hancock, "Watermelon Man," re-mix, 1973 Grover Washington, "Mister Magic," 1975
Smooth	1980s Joe Sample, "Street Life," 1979 "One Day, I'll Fly Away," 1980
Faith-based	1990–2000s Kirk Whalum, "Falling in Love with Jesus," 2002
Hip-Hop	2010s Robert Glasper, "Gonna Be Alright," 2012

The RAP Year Book: The Most Important Rap Song from Every Year Since 1979, Discussed, Debated, and Deconstructed
by Shea Serrano

1979	"Rapper's Delight"	The Sugarhill Gang
1980	"The Breaks"	Kurtis Blow
1981	"Jazzy Sensation"	Afrika Bambaataa and Jazzy Five
1982	"The Message"	Grandmaster Flash and Furious Five
1983	"Sucker M.C.s"	Run-DMC
1984	"Friends"	Whodini
1985	"La Di Da Di"	Doug E. Fresh and Slick Rick
1986	"6 in the Mornin'"	Ice-T
1987	"Paid in Full"	Eric B. and Rakim
1988	"Straight Outta Compton"	N.W.A.
1989	"Fight the Power"	Public Enemy
1990	"Bonita Applebum"	A Tribe Called Quest
1991	"Mind Playing Tricks on Me"	Geto Boys
1992	"Nuthin' but a 'G' Thang"	Dr. Dre feat. Snoop Dogg

1993	"C.R.E.A.M."	Wu-Tang Clan
1994	"Juicy"	The Notorious B.I.G.
1995	"Dear Mama"	Tupac
1996	"California Love"	Tupac (Dr. Dre and Roger Troutman)
1997	"Can't Nobody Hold Me Down"	Puff Daddy feat. Mase
1998	"Ruff Ryders' Anthem"	DMX
1999	"My Name Is"	Eminem
2000	"Big Pimpin"	Jay-Z feat. UGK
2001	"Takeover" vs "Ether"	Jay-Z vs Nas
2002	"Grindin'"	Clipse
2003	"In Da Club"	50 Cent
2004	"Still Tippin'"	Mike Jones (Slim Thug and Paul Wall)
2005	"Gold Digger"	Kanye West feat. Jamie Foxx
2006	"Hustlin'"	Rick Ross
2007	"International Players Anthem"	UGK feat. Outkast
2008	"A Milli"	Lil Wayne
2009	"Best I Ever Had"	Drake
2010	"Monster"	Kanye West (Rick Ross, Jay Z, Bon Iver, and Nicki Minaj)
2011	"Niggas in Paris"	Jay Z and Kanye West
2012	"Same Love"	Macklemore and Ryan Lewis
2013	"Control"	Big Sean (Kendrick Lamar and Jay Electronica)
2014	"Lifestyle"	Rich Gang (Young Thug and Rich Homie Quan)

Glossary of Terms

aesthetic: the quality of nature and beauty; arts

Afrocentric (or African-centric): Afrocentric artists identify Africa as the source for Black aesthetics, ideals, practices, and social order.

akonting: a folk lute from the Jola people of Senegambia; is a clear predecessor to the American Negro banjo and has a similar playing style.

anthem: the traditional meaning of the term *anthem* is a specific form of angelic church music, but the more general understanding is a celebratory song used as a symbol for a particular group of people.

áse (or áshe): means "so be it," "may it happen."

backbeat: a sharp attack on beats two and four in a 4/4 metered measure.

bebop: the jazz genre of the 1940s that featured small ensembles, jam sessions, improvisations, fast tempos, complex chord structures, and innovative harmonies.

Black: refers to people of the African diaspora (e.g. African Americans, Jamaicans, Cubans), who share a heritage dominantly from the western central or southern regions of Africa.

Black Power movement: the Black Power movement was inspired by the philosophy of Black nationalism which advocated self-sufficiency, self-control, and full participation in the decision-making process on issues affecting the lives of Black people.

blues: the culture of storytelling through music, and the foundation of American popular music

call and response: the verbal or nonverbal alternation between a leader and participatory audience.

capoeira: a fightlike dance created by enslaved Africans in Brazil that mixes elements of martial arts, dance, folklore, sport, ritual, and training for unarmed fighting.

chorus: a lyric statement following the verse that is often repeated periodically throughout the song, usually with the same lyrics and melody.

community: a group of interacting people living in close location to each other; with shared or common values.

community building: a field of practice directed toward the creation or enhancement of community between individuals within a regional area or common interest.

community engagement: the process of relationship building that encourages learning and action, as well as the expression of ideas and opinions about a given issue or program.

culture: the changing pattern of human knowledge, belief, and behavior learned and transmitted through generations.

diaspora: the breaking up and scattering of a people who had to settle far from their ancestral homeland.

dinza: (jazz) the Ki-Kongo verb *dinza,* to discharge one's semen, to come

DJ: literally, disc jockey. The one who played the songs—eventually called turntablism

eckankar: coworker with God; a new religious movement founded by Paul Twicher

folktale: a characteristically anonymous and timeless tale circulated orally among a people.

freedom songs: spiritual lyrics transformed by the activist song leaders, traditional melodies used, and methods associated with old forms that were blended with new forms to create songs with the force and intent.

funk: a musical genre characterized by group singing, complex polyrhythmic structures, percussive instrumental and vocal timbres, and a featured horn section. (Funk/R and B considered the closest source of music that resembles the original drum sounds from Africa.)

gig: a music job or performance for pay

gospel style: improvised and melismatic vocal style characterized by a strained, full-throated sound, and emotion-religious lyrics.

griot (or jelis/jalis): an African storyteller-musician. The griot (the more common colonialist French term) or jeli (the indigenous Mande term)

harmony: can imply that the melody is layered with other voices or instruments, presenting one or more tonal sounds along with the line; two or more musical notes produced or sounded at the same time.

hip-hop: competitive cultural expressions of urban youth, including graffiti artist, mobile DJs, breakers (b-boys, b-girls, break-dancers), and MCs (later known as rappers). It provided both entertainment and a forum for competitive, nonviolent gang warfare. By the 1990s, hip-hop or rap music was used to mean any R and B and pop music that incorporated rapping or DJing production.

humanities: The art of being human; the investigation and study of the arts

jazz: considered art music or classical music that is to be studied.

kora: a stringed harplike instrument played in Guinea, Guinea-Bissau, Mali, Senegal, Burkina Faso, and the Gambia by the jeli (jali) or griot.

melody: a phrase or line that can be sung or played by an instrument; a song or tune; a succession of musical notes or pitches that seem to have a relation to one another and express a musical thought.

minstrelsy: the first indigenous American theatrical and popular music genre, popular in the 1800s; a variety showed based on crude and racist stereotypes of African Americans.

moaning: or referred to as a *gospel moan* is full of emotion and meaning, including a resonance which is more than a physical sound.

music: organized sound; the design of sound and silence, which include rhythm, melody and harmony

nommo: meaning "word" or word seed

ragtime: A late 1800s piano-based music mixing complex syncopated rhythms with traditional European musical forms.

revolutionary: a person who is committed and works for or engaging in political struggle and conflict.

rhythm: gives the song a beat, or meter, to initiate movement; the arrangement of time in music.

rhythm and blues (R and B): a name originally used in the late 1940s and early 1950s to describe African American popular music in general.

ring shout: considered by some as an early Negro *holy dance* in which circling about is the essential prime element.

shaman: often referred to as a healer; they have the ability to *see* visions, travel between physical and spiritual realms, and transform energy.

social justice: is a concept of fair and just relations between the individual and society; how the distribution of wealth, opportunities, and privileges within a society.

song: in music, usually is a composition for voice or voices, performed by singing

soul: (music) originally one of the jazz styles started in the 1960s; meaningful and conscious singing and music; has an emotional gospel evolution as well. Soul is a concept, aesthetic, and sensibility that embodies the ideology of the Black Power movement. It echoes the voices of college-aged students who rejected the integrationist philosophy of the 1950s civil rights leaders for the nationalist ideology of Black nationalism.

spirit: from the Latin *spiritus*, which means "breath," and from a Proto-Indo-European *(s)peis*, which implies the *soul.*

spirituals: essential expressions of social strivings and struggle whose themes are: 1) the desire for freedom, justice, and penalty for the oppressor; 2) criticism of the existing order; and 3) coded messages of escape, meetings, and struggle

story: the element of music that combines all the other components to evoke a deep feeling or emotion.

storytelling: the art of narrative performance.

swing: African-derived triplet-based rhythmic feel often encouraged in jazz, blues, and R and B. A typical swing rhythm can be approximated by taking a series of even   beats, then lengthening the first and shortening the second beat to create a sequence of pairs of long and short notes.

tradition: a temporal concept that entangles the past with the present and affects or creates the future. Tradition involves practicing love and passing it from one generation to the next, from one environment to another. Tradition is the "changing same" (Baraka, 1966).

trickster: a clever character (human or animal in a folk narrative tradition) who is able to manipulate others to get what he or she wants.

work song: African-derived music sung by workers in rhythm with their work; often a call and response in which a lead singer acting as a foreman sings a lyric to direct the work, then workers answer and perform the required task.

References

Afrika, Llaila O. *African Holistic Health* (Buffalo, NY: EWORLD INC, 2004).

Albertson, Chris. "Bessie Smith: Empress of the Blues," (catalog notes) Sony Music Foundation, New York, 1991.

Allen, N.T. Exploring Hip-Hop Therapy with high-risk youth. *Praxis: School of Social Work Journal*, 5 30–36, 2005.

Allen, William Francis, Pickard, Charles, and Garrison, Lucy. *Slave Songs of the United States*. New York: A. Simpson & Co, 1867.

Aluede, Charles O. "Music Therapy in Traditional African Societies: Origin, basis and application in Nigeria." J. Hum. Ecol., 20(1): 31–35, 2006.

Alvarez III, T.T. *Beats, Rhymes and Life: Exploring the use of Rap Therapy with urban adolescents.* Unpublished master's thesis, Smith College School for Social Work, Northampton, MA, 2006.

Apel, Willi. *Harvard Brief Dictionary of Music* (Cambridge, MA: Washington Square Press, 1961).

Bebey, Francis. *African Music: A people's art* (NY: Lawrence Hill & Company, 1975).

Belafonte, Harry. *Long Road to Freedom: An anthology of Black Music* (New York: Buddha Records, 2001).

Bennett, C.I. *Comprehensive Multicultural Education: Theory and Practice*, 6th ed. (Boston, MA: Allyn & Bacon, 2006).

Bhutia, Thinley Kalsang. *Invalidated site: Cleansings and Ewe Orisa Esu*. May 11, 2015

Bond, Julian and Wilson, Sondra Kathryn. *Lift Every Voice and Sing: A celebration of the Negro National Anthem, 100 years, 100 Voices* (New York: Random House, 2000).

Brauneis, Robert. "Copyright and the World's Most Popular Song." *GWU Legal Studies Research Paper No. 1111624*, 2010.

Campbell, Lisa. *Michael Jackson: The king of pop's darkest hour* (Wellesley, MA: Branden Publishing Company, 1994).

Chang, Jeff. *Can't Stop Won't Stop: A History of the Hip-Hop Generation* (New York: Picador St. Martin's Press, 2005).

Cleveland, James. *Songs of Zion: Supplemental worship* (Nashville, TN: Abingdon Press, 1981).

Coffman, Don. "Common ground for community music and music education." International Journal of Community Music, Volume 6 Number 3, University of Miami, 2013.

Coplan, David B. and Jules-Rosette, Bennetta. "Nkosi Sikelel' iAfrika and the Liberation of the Spirit of South Africa." African Studies, 64, 2, December 2005.

Costa, A. L. and Kallick, B. *Discovering and Exploring Habits of Mind* (Association for Supervision and Curriculum Development, 2000).

Crowe, Barbara J. *Music and Soulmaking: Toward a New Theory of Music Therapy* (Lanham, MD: Scarecrow Press, 2004).

DeCarlo, A. and Hockman, E. Rap Therapy: A group work intervention method for urban adolescents. *Social Work with Groups,* 26, 45–59, 2003.

Delpit Lisa. *Other People's Children: Cultural conflict in the Classroom* (New York: The New Press, 1996).

Doumbia, Adama. *The Way of the Elders: West African Spirituality & Traditions* (Saint Paul, Minn: Llewellyn Publications, 2004).

Evans, Freddi Williams. *Congo Square: African Roots in New Orleans* (New Orleans: University of Louisiana at Lafayette Press, 2011).

Floyd, Samuel, Jr. *Power of Black Music* (New York: Oxford University Press, 1995).

Friedman, Robert Lawrence. *The Healing Power of the Drum* (Gilsum, NH: White Cliffs Media, 2000).

Gioa, Ted. *Healing Songs* (Durham, NC: Duke University Press, 2006).

Hadley, S and Yancy, G. (editors). *Therapeutic Uses of Rap and Hip-Hop* (NY: Routledge, 2012).

Haltiwanger, John. *Elite Daily*. How Kendrick Lamar is proof hip-hop can influence society in big ways. August 3, 2015.

Hall, James. *The Art of Song* (Norman, OK: University of Oklahoma Press, 1953).

Hester, Karlton E. *From Africa to Afrocentric Innovations Some Call "Jazz"* (NY: Hesteria Records and Publishing Company, 2000).

Hindley, Geoffrey. *The Lacrousse Encyclopedia of Music*. Book Sales, 1971.

Hodgson, Kimberly. "Community Engagement: How Art and Cultural Strategies Enhance Community Engagement" (*This briefing paper from APA's Planning and Community Health Research Center) http://www.planning.org/research/arts/briefing papers/engagement.htm, 2013*.

Ho, P., Tsao, J.C.I., Bloch, L., and Zeltzer, L. K. The impact of group drumming on social-emotional behavior in low-income children. *Evidence-based complementary and alternative medicine*, Article ID 250708, Berkeley, CA http://dx.doi.org/10.1093/ecam/neq072, 2011.

Huray, Peter Le. "Anthem" in Stanley Sadie, ed. *The New Grove Dictionary of Music and Musicians* (London: Macmillan Press, 1980).

Jahn, Janheinz. *Muntu: The New African Culture* (Germany: Faber and Faber, 1958).

Jirousek, Charlotte. 1995. "Rhythm." *In an Interactive Textbook*, Ithaca: Cornell University website -- (http://char.txa.cornell.edu/language/principl/rhythm/rhythm.htm).

Jones, LeRoi. *Blues People: The Negro Experience in White America and the Music That Developed from It* (NY: Morrow and Company, 1963).

Karenga, Maulana. *Introduction to Black Studies* (Los Angeles, CA: The University of Sankore Press, 2002).

Kitwana, Bakari. *The Hip-Hop Generation: Young Blacks and the Crisis in African- American Culture* (NY: Perseus Books Group).

Kouyate, D'Jimo. "The Role of the Griot," in *Talk That Talk: An Anthology of African-American Storytelling*, eds. Linda Goss and Marian E. Barnes (NY: Simon and Schuster/Touchstone,

1989), pp. 179–81. KQED, http://www.pbs.org/black-culture/explore/black-authors-spoken-word-poetry/lift-every-voice-and-sing/), 2013.

La Vere, Stephen C. "Robert Johnson," (catalog notes for) Columbia Records Inc., New York, 1990.

Lamar, K. (2017). *Damn.* Los Angeles, California, United States of America: Top Dawg Entertainment, Aftermath Entertainment Legg, Andrew. "A Taxonomy of Musical Gestures in African American Gospel Music." *Popular Music*, Volume 29 (1) Jan 2010, pp. 103–129

Levine, Lawrence W. *Black Culture and Black Consciousness: Afro-American folk thought from slavery to freedom* (Oxford, England: Oxford University Press, 1977).

Library of Congress. (http://www.loc.gov/teachers/lyrical/songs/overcome.html), 2013.

Lighthouse, A. *Yo! Can ya flow?: A qualitative study of hip-hop aesthetics and original rap lyrics created in-group music therapy in an urban youth shelter.* Unpublished master's research, 2004. Available at https://www.wlu.ca/soundeffects/researchablelibrary/Aaron.pdf

Lynch, Joe. *Billboard Bulletin.* Pulitzer prize administrator explains how Kendrick Lamar won. April 17, 2018.

Mannes, Elena. *The Power of Music: Pioneering discoveries in the science of song* (New York: Walker Publishing, 2011).

Margolick, David, and Als. Hilton. *Strange Fruit: The Biography of a Song* (Paperback ed., 2001) Ecco ISBN 0-06-095956-8.

Mason, John Edwin. "Mannenberg": Notes on the making of an icon and anthem. African Studies Quarterly, Volume 9, Issue 4, Fall, 2007.

Maultsby, Portia. "The Crisis Interview with Portia Maultsby on Black Music," *Crisis Magazine*, February 2005, Cleveland, Ohio.

McClellan, R. *The Healing Forces of Music* (New York: Amity House Inc., 1988.

Mithen, Steven. *The Singing Neanderthals: The Origins of Music, Language, Mind, and Body* (London: Weidenfeld & Nicholson, 2005).

Neal, Mark Anthony. *Songs in the Key of Black Life: A Rhythm and Blues Nation* (New York: Routledge, 2003).

Nunez, Sal. *Medicinal Drumming: An Ancient and Modern Day Healing Approach.* NeuroQuantology. June 2016, Vol 14(2), pp. 226–241.

Perry, T., Steele, P., and Hilliard, A. *Young, Gifted, and Black: Promoting High Achievement among African-American Students* (Boston, MA: Beacon Press, 2003).

Petchauer, Emery. *Hip-Hop Culture in College Students' Lives: Elements, embodiment, and higher edutainment* (New York: Routledge, 2012).

Peterson, M. S. Strategies for effective oral communication. In L.B. Gallen Jr. and M.S. Peterson (Eds). *Instructing and mentoring the African American college student: Strategies for success in higher education*, pp. 69–83 (Boston, MA: Allyn & Bacon, 2004).

Ramsey, Gunthrie P. *Race Music: Black Cultures from Bebop to Hip-Hop* (Berkeley, CA: University Press, 2003).

Reagon, Bernice. The Black Music Research Journal, Volume 7, 1987; in Guy and Candie Carawan, "Sing For Freedom: The Story of the Civil Rights Movement Through Its Songs," (Bethlehem, PA: Sing Out Corp., 1990, p. 5).

Redmond, Shana L. *Anthem: Social Movements and the Sound of Solidarity in the African Diaspora.* (NY: New York University Press, 2014).

Robbins, Nordoff. The Guardian. *How Music Acts as a Medicine for the Soul.* Thursday, 28 Jun 2012.

Rocha, Diego A. *The Cupola: Scholarship at Gettysburg College.* Kendrick Lamar and hip-hop as medium for social change. Spring 2017.

Ruud, E. *Music Therapy: Improvisation, Communication, and Culture* (NH: Barcelona Gilsum, 1998).

Sanger, Kerran, L. *When the Spirit Says Sing: The Role of Freedom Songs in the Civil Rights Movement* (NY: Garland Publishing, 1995).

Scorsese, Martin. "The Blues: A Documentary Film Series" (liner notes) PBS Broadcasting, 2003.

Serrano, Shea. *The Rap Year Book: The Most Important Rap Song From Every Year Since 1979, Discussed, Debated, and Deconstructed* (NY: Abrams Image, 2015).

Stevens, Christine. *The Art and Heart of Drum Circles* (Milwaukee, MI: Hal Leonard Corp., 2003).

Stevens, Denis. *A History of Song* (Connecticut: Greenwood, 1960).

Stige, B. *Culture-Centered Music Therapy* ((NH: Barcelona Gilsum, 2002).

Tutu, Desmond. Goodreads. (http://www.goodreads.com/quotes/132842-a-person-is-a-person-through-other-persons-none-of).

Tyson, E.H. Rap music in social work practice with African-American and Latino youth: A conceptual model with practical applications. *Journal of Human Behavior in the Social Environment, 8(4), 1–21, 2003.*

Vincent, Rickey. *Party Music: The Inside Story of the Black Panthers' Band and How Black Power Transformed Soul Music* (Chicago: Lawrence Hill Books, 2013).

Ward, Brian. "People Get Ready": Music and the Civil Rights Movement of the 1950s and 1960s (http://www.gilderlehrman.org/history-by-era/civil-rights-movement/essays/"people-get-ready"-music-and-civil-rights-movement-1950s), 2012.

We Are the World USA for Africa Book (Perigee Books, 1985).

Werner, Craig. *A Change Is Gonna Come: Music, Race & the Soul of America* (New York, NY: Published by the Penguin Group, 1998).

About the Author

$\mathcal{D}$r. Terence Elliott is an educator with more than thirty years of teaching experience. He is an accomplished pianist, composer, and producer. He earned a doctorate in educational leadership from Argosy University in 2010, and holds a master's degree in creative arts and a bachelor's degree in music and Black studies that he earned at San Francisco State University. He is a former academic dean, president of the academic senate, and chair of the African American studies at Contra Costa College. Currently, he works as a full-time music professor, teaching rock, rhythm, and blues, and hip-hop courses at Diablo Valley College (DVC) in Northern California. He is a board member on the A2MEND (African American Male Educational Network Development) organization, and co-leads the African American Male Leadership Program at DVC.

A proud husband of thirty-five years and father of two beautiful (and married) daughters, two fantastic sons-in-law, and an awesome granddaughter, Dr. Terence Elliott hopes to use his music as a way to bring community together through his own particular *cycle of life* journey of love, pain, hope, change, and healing.